Cambridge Elements ≡

Elements in the Global Middle Ages
edited by
Geraldine Heng
University of Texas at Austin
Susan J. Noakes
University of Minnesota–Twin Cities
Lynn Ramey
Vanderbilt University

ELEPHANTS AND IVORY IN CHINA AND SPAIN

John Beusterien
Texas Tech University
Stephen West
University of California, Berkeley

CAMBRIDGE
UNIVERSITY PRESS

Shaftesbury Road, Cambridge CB2 8EA, United Kingdom

One Liberty Plaza, 20th Floor, New York, NY 10006, USA

477 Williamstown Road, Port Melbourne, VIC 3207, Australia

314–321, 3rd Floor, Plot 3, Splendor Forum, Jasola District Centre,
New Delhi – 110025, India

103 Penang Road, #05–06/07, Visioncrest Commercial, Singapore 238467

Cambridge University Press is part of Cambridge University Press & Assessment,
a department of the University of Cambridge.

We share the University's mission to contribute to society through the pursuit of
education, learning and research at the highest international levels of excellence.

www.cambridge.org
Information on this title: www.cambridge.org/9781009507455

DOI: 10.1017/9781009172578

First published 2025

A catalogue record for this publication is available from the British Library

ISBN 978-1-009-50745-5 Hardback
ISBN 978-1-009-17256-1 Paperback
ISSN 2632-3427 (online)
ISSN 2632-3419 (print)

Elephants and Ivory in China and Spain

Elements in the Global Middle Ages

DOI: 10.1017/9781009172578
First published online: January 2025

John Beusterien
Texas Tech University

Stephen West
University of California, Berkeley

Author for correspondence: John Beusterien, john.beusterien@ttu.edu

Abstract: This Element provides a global history of ivory and elephants, acknowledging the individuality and dignity of the elephants that provided that ivory. Sections on China include the first translations of texts about the cultural importance of elephants and ivory in the Song Dynasty (960–1279) and an examination of an ivory stave (*huban* 笏板), crafted from an Asian elephant tusk (*Elephas maximus*), carried by officials in court and other formal rituals. Sections on Spain examine the value of ivory during the reign of King Alfonso X of Castile (1221–84) and the Virxe Abrideira (ca. 1260–75), an ivory Virgin and Child statuette owned by Queen Violante of Aragon (1236–1301), crafted from an African elephant tusk (*Loxodonta africana*). The Element concludes by offering a pedagogy from a comparative literature perspective about *Sunjata* (ca. 1226), an epic from the Mali empire in West Africa, an important source for thirteenth-century global ivory markets.

This Element also has a video abstract: www.cambridge.org/Beusterien

Keywords: Elephants, Ivory, China, Spain, African literature

ISBNs: 9781009507455 (HB), 9781009172561 (PB), 9781009172578 (OC)
ISSNs: 2632-3427 (online), 2632-3419 (print)

Contents

1 Introduction   1

2 A Global History   5

3 Elephants in China   13

4 Ivory in China and a Stave   42

5 Elephants and Ivory in Iberia   50

6 A Virgin and Child Statuette   62

7 *Sunjata*   86

8 Conclusion   90

   Notes about the Text   93

   References   94

1 Introduction

Elephants walk a lot during their lives. And breathe. They feel things deeply, like the loss of a loved one. When the earth's largest terrestrial land mammals mourn, they can express delicate feelings of empathy through vocalized pain and distress. They may even call out the "name" of the individual who has passed away, because wild elephants address one another with individually specific calls (Pardo et al. 2024).

Sometimes, when an elephant is dying from sickness or wounds, other elephants may gather around and try to lift or feed their ailing companion. Elephants often pay tribute to friends and family members that have passed by touching the remains with their trunk; they may then cover them with leaves and branches and hold vigil with the remains for multiple days. They may pass around the bones of dead elephants. Some even die of grief if a companion elephant dies.

Because of the success of conservation efforts, or perhaps because their images are ubiquitous, people sometimes believe that a sizeable number of elephants share the planet with humans. If one considers the land on earth where elephants can roam, however, the proportion of land for elephant habitats versus that dedicated to livestock animals or human settlements is minuscule. If one considers the mass of all living land mammals, the mammal biomass of humans is 390 metric tons and that of the earth's livestock, overwhelmingly dominated by cattle, is 630 metric tons. In radical contrast, the land mass of all wild animals is 22 metric tons and that of all living wild elephants is 1.3 metric tons. In other words, the combined weight of humans and cattle is about 785 times heavier than all living wild elephants. The total biomass of domestic cats alone is almost double that of the African savannah elephant (Greenspoon et al. 2023).

Since Hannibal's march into Rome, elephants have been the stuff of legends in world history. As opposed to the Roman classical period, however, elephants were, for the most part, not used in battle in the Middle Ages. Nonetheless, medieval Europe cherished the legend of battle elephants, and medieval Eurasia more broadly desired the acquisition of live elephants. China successfully imported hundreds of elephants from the ninth to the fourteenth century, in radical contrast to Europe, which imported only three during the same period. But neither Europeans, nor the Chinese, ever used elephants in battle in the medieval period.

Moreover, after the extinction of the northern African variety that Hannibal and the Romans used in warfare, the only variety of live elephants transported in the Middle Ages (all the way up until the nineteenth century) were Asian elephants. African elephants in the medieval period were not used for work or war. They, however, were killed for ivory. African ivory was the most valued. It was processed from elephants slaughtered in hunts.

Many types of elephants have lived through the ages. In recent geological history, elephants were reduced to the Asian (*Elephas maximus*) and African (*Loxodonta africana*) varieties, both of which have three subspecies. Many early Elephantidae species died off because of changes of climate and subsequent habitat alteration, but, by far, humans have been the primary agent of elephant decimation over the last 10,000 years. Pre-agricultural cultures killed elephants for their meat, and their ivory was a by-product of hunting; by the Middle Ages, ivory was no longer a by-product but was valued to such a degree that elephant tusks were the end product of the hunt, for markets far away from the animal's original habitat.

This Element introduces the reader to elephants and ivory in the Middle Ages, with a special focus on Iberia and China. It does not assume the reader has previous knowledge about elephants and ivory sculpting, nor about Spanish and Chinese medieval history. We hope that the study will be a springboard for a host of other yet-to-be-determined studies such as the use of live elephants in war in Southeast Asia, ivory networks to the Mughal or Ottoman empires, or the history of human and elephant relationships in sub-Saharan Africa.

Aside from a historical overview of elephants and ivory, the Element focuses on the lives of two previously unnamed elephants from world history whose tusks were extracted when trade in elephant ivory was booming. To provide a context for the discussion of elephants and ivory in medieval China and Spain, Section 2 offers a global history of elephants and the importance of their ivory. It underscores the importance of African elephants as the preferred ivory source in the Middle Ages and the significance of the Vedic period (the late Bronze and early Iron Age in the history of India, ca. 1500–500 BCE) for the history of Asian elephants, the only species that humans held in captivity up until the twentieth century that survives today. Section 2 also describes the North African species which humans drove to extinction.

Sections 3 and 4 focus on the Song Dynasty (960–1279). In Section 3, texts are presented that describe the capture of live elephants; the exportation of those animals from Vietnam to China as tribute animals; the institutionalization of care, feeding, and lodging; the pain that captive elephants experienced; and their adornment and participation in processions for imperial rituals. Texts also describe the hunting of elephants. Section 4 examines the history of ivory in China and a thirteenth-century stave (*huban* 笏), a narrow flat strip of ivory like a stick or wand held in court and other formal rituals by civil bureaucrats and in use for two millennia. In Section 4, the authors also imagine a possible scenario for a biogeography of the elephant that provided the material to make the stave.

Sections 5 and 6 focus on the history of King Alfonso X of Castile (1221–84) and Queen Violante of Aragon (1236–1301). In contrast to the hundreds of live elephants brought to China under the Song Dynasty, Section 5 points out that no live elephants were brought to Spain in the thirteenth century and describes the only three brought alive to Europe from the ninth to the fourteenth century. Although he had no live elephant to fight, the section also examines how King Alfonso X literally and symbolically used ivory as a sign in battles with Islamic forces.

Section 6 examines an example of elephant ivory belonging to King Alfonso's wife, Queen Violante. Violante once owned the Virxe Abrideira (ca. 1260–75), an ivory Virgin and Child statuette found today in the town of Allariz. The analysis of Queen Violante's statuette is presented as a history in reverse, detailing in reverse chronological order a plausible course from its arrival in Spain back to the tusk extracted from a hunted sub-Saharan elephant.

The methodology for the study of China is philological. It focuses on written historical sources translated for the first time into English that describe the administration and history of live elephants used in official processions in the Song Dynasty. The methodology for the sections dedicated to Iberia relies on literature, history, art history, anthropology, and other disciplines. The scholarship establishes a tactile history from a queen's object of worship back to the extraction of the African elephant tooth. Despite the different approaches – a philological methodology versus a multidisciplinary historical approach – the sections devoted to China and Spain both offer shared themes. In Spain and China, elephants and their ivory were important to international diplomacy and associated with the power of kingship.

Many are familiar with the elephant's name "Jumbo," a name filled with cultural insensitivity (a derivative word taken from a greeting used by Swahili language traders from Southeast Africa). The original Jumbo was a zoo captive made orphan by the nineteenth-century global ivory trade (Nance 2015). But modern zoos and circuses were not the first to name captive elephants. Alexander the Great, perhaps mimicking Indian practices, dedicated an elephant to the sun. Alexander named the elephant Ajax (Ng 2019: 104). Hannibal named his favorite elephant Syros. In the imperial capital in western Germany, Charlemagne received a live elephant as a diplomatic gift from Baghdad whom he named Abū al-ʿAbbās. Third Little Girl was a captive elephant that performed during the Song Dynasty. Ortelão (Peppermint) worked on the fifteenth-century docks in southern India at the port of Colombo hauling lumber and loading goods onto ships bound for Portugal in the West and Macau in the Far East (Jordan Gschwend 2010: 50). Hanno, the famed white elephant, was a Portuguese diplomatic gift in the fifteenth century to Pope Leo X (Bedini

1998). Akbar, Mughal emperor in India, gave the name Hawa'i (Skyrocket) to a particularly fierce elephant in his menagerie (Kistler 2006: 210).

Instead of studying historical elephants bestowed with names, the authors of this Element engage in the methodology of biogeography by studying two elephants whom history never deemed worthy of a name. By naming two elephants who never received a name in history, that is, in naming previously anonymous elephants, the authors call attention to the historic practice of naming captive elephants, which often included a life of torment in which they were taken away from their communities, caged, or chained, and sometimes kept distressed or depressed for the rest of their lives.

Most directly, the creative act of naming elephants forgotten in history calls attention to the individuality of the two elephants killed for the ivory provided for a Chinese stave and an Iberian statuette. The Vietnamese name "Y Khun" is given for the Asian elephant that provided the ivory for the stave. The Mande name "Kouyaté" is given for the African elephant whose tusk was shaped into the statuette. In coining a name for two thirteenth-century elephants that supplied ivory artifacts, the authors also call attention to how medieval cultures painted the culture that supplied its ivory in disparaging terms and how the cultures that consumed ivory ignored the life of torment to which elephant populations were subjected before their tusks were put in global markets.

Art historians long only studied the "thing," that is, the carved ivory object itself, disregarding the life of elephants and the ivory supply network. In naming two elephants, this Element takes a cue from an art historian and a museum curator. The art historian Sarah Guérin (2015b) studies the carved ivory object beyond its life as thing. Guérin's study of the Salerno ivories (a collection of plaques with narrative scenes from the Bible and the largest set of ivory carvings preserved from the pre-Gothic Middle Ages) reconstructs the history of the elephant that provided the ivory. Ashley Coutu, research curator of African archeology at the Pitt Rivers Museum in Oxford, studies ivory through the life of an individual elephant killed by poachers in nineteenth-century East Africa through combining isotopic analysis with archival information such as explorer accounts, trade records, and photographs (Coutu 2015).

Like the studies from these two scholars, we establish a connection to a real animal. The biogeography – that is, an object biography and naming of two elephants – is an act of reclamation that joins the spirit of the studies by Guérin and Coutu which focus on the individuality of elephants. The "biogeography" (instead of biography) methodology adds to their approaches in that it names the individual to recognize the original natural habitat and the human-created networks that altered the location of the animal and their remains from their origins (Beusterien 2020b; Beusterien 2023).

We conclude the Element by suggesting a pedagogy based on our research: a comparative literature approach is presented for connecting the global history of elephants and ivory to the study of *Sunjata*, first composed in the thirteenth century (ca. 1226). *Sunjata* is an epic from the West African Mali empire, an important source for global ivory markets, including China and Spain.

2 A Global History

The most powerful potentates in Eurasia in the thirteenth century cherished the gift of a live elephant because the animal symbolized the power of kingliness. Global princes also demanded elephant ivory because of its exquisite qualities, aesthetically and materially. The supply of live elephants versus ivory were met, for the most part, by different breeds. In the Middle Ages, up until the end of the eighteenth century, the only live elephants that were moved across great distances were Asian elephants. In turn, the same global powers, from western Europe to China, all got what they considered the best ivory from the same place: African elephants from the sub-Sahara.

Thousands of elephant tusks were used throughout Eurasia in the Middle Ages, and markets preferred those from sub-Saharan Africa. In the thirteenth century, the supply of ivory tusks previously sourced from East Africa had dwindled, and demands for elephant ivory were supplied by new routes crossing the Sahara in camel caravans from Central and West Africa (Guérin 2013; Guérin 2019; Guérin 2022: 11). The following section presents a global history of ivory and elephants to provide a historical context for the ivory networks and the live elephants that supplied medieval China and Spain.

Many animals supplied medieval cultures with ivory. Carvers in China sometimes extracted well-preserved ivory from the remains of woolly mammoths (*Mammuthus primigenius*), most likely found in the northern tundra. One Buddhist sculpture, likely from the Southern Song Dynasty in China, uses mammoth ivory to depict the founder of Buddhism, Shakyamuni, with attendant bodhisattvas (Figure 1). This was not the first time that humans had carved mammoth tusks. Statuettes of a male and a female reindeer swimming (now located in the British Museum, accession number Palart 550) and a man in the shape of a lion (now in the Ulm Museum in Germany) are from prehistoric cultures that hunted mammoths and carved their tusks. The thirteenth-century Buddhist sculptures, though, demonstrate that the appetite in China for ivory was so high that ivory was sought out and acquired even from the remains of the then-extinct mammoth.

Ivory in the Middle Ages was also sourced from narwhals (*Monodon monoceros*). The toothed whale lives in the Arctic, and its long, spiraling tusk can

Figure 1 Buddha Shakyamuni with attendant bodhisattvas from China. End of thirteenth century. Medium: mammoth ivory. Dimensions: height 23.5 cm. Metropolitan Museum of Art, New York, accession number: 34.26.1a, b–3a, b. Open access CC0.

grow more than ten feet in length. The Greenland Norse, perhaps trading with Indigenous hunters like the Thule (the predecessors of the modern Inuit and Yupik groups), made the tusks available in global markets, where the tooth was popularly assumed to be a unicorn's horn. Elites safeguarded narwhal teeth in collections and churches from London to Kraków (Malcolm 2022). Sometimes, the narwhal horn was carved into a goblet or ground into a powder. As with rhinoceros horns, drinking from the horn, or literally drinking the horn itself in powdered form, was believed to have curative properties. Unlike rhinoceros horns, which are made up of keratin, the same substance as human hair and fingernails, the narwhal's horn is an extended tooth made from dentine, virtually the same chemical composition as an elephant or mammoth's tusk.

Walrus ivory was also frequently used in northern Europe in the Middle Ages, where it was extracted from as far away as North America (Barrow 2021; Frei et al. 2015; Star et al. 2018). In the same way that they were typically unaware of an object's narwhal provenance, so people were unaware of the walrus provenance of ivory objects. For instance, people who regarded a medieval crucifix would not have known that artists used ivory from different animals for the same sculpture. One thirteenth-century Crucified Christ (now in the Herlufsholm Church in Denmark) contains elephant ivory for his crucified curved body and walrus ivory for his arms.

Despite the *longue durée* of carving ivory (as well as bones) from all sorts of animals, elephants were humanity's favored ivory source in the Middle Ages. Ivory is of much higher quality than bone, and artists chose elephant ivory over the less finely grained ivory substitutes from other animals because of its superior quality. Given the choice between an Asian and African elephant, the only two species that survived into the medieval period, global markets preferred ivory from Africa. Only males of the Asian elephant variety grow tusks, and their tusks are relatively smaller than those from Africa. Art historian Sarah Guérin states the key distinguishing feature as to why size was the preference: the African tusk is much thicker than the Asian. The added material around the nerve center enables the carving of larger ivory objects. (2022: 8).

Whereas elephant species in the Americas disappeared as the result of climate and human hunting, elephants survived alongside humans in Africa. Prior to the seventeenth century, sub-Saharan human communities did not hunt elephants toward pell-mell destruction as happened in so many parts of the world where humans settled. Agropastoralism in savannah rangelands was compatible with elephants, and with wildlife more broadly. The Maasai, for instance, who occupied the extensive rangelands of Amboseli, lived alongside elephants for hundreds, if not thousands, of years (Kangwana and Browne-Núñez 2011: 31).

One clue to understanding sub-Saharan African cohabitation with elephants is evidenced by nineteenth-century colonialism. Britain, to shore up elephant services for the empire, exported Indian elephants to Africa for draft work. The project failed when Britain did not bring in mahouts with the animals. In turn, King Leopold II of Belgium (1865–1909), who had seen elephants in Sri Lanka (Ceylon) in 1879, moved four Indian elephants with thirteen mahouts to the Belgian Congo with a plan of initiating an elephant-based transport service under the control of a cavalry officer (Shell 2015: 46). The colonial hiring of mahouts out of Asia in sub-Saharan Africa gives evidence of European efforts to impose a model of taming elephants. In the attempt to transfer the Indian paradigm onto Africa, colonial powers like that of Leopold ignored the complex elephant kin relationships that had afforded a long-term communal land-tenure ecology between humans and animals in the sub-Sahara.

Whereas cattle are an animal domestication success story, elephants are a story of failure. In contrast to cattle, elephants never entered a lasting breeding regime in human history because they were not economic. Elephant gestation is two years, and elephants typically only give birth to one calf at a time. They eat and drink an enormous amount and are unable to work for humans until fourteen years of age. Financing a tame elephant also means funding a long-term human handler and food.

Never fully molding them into domesticates, humans only had marginal success in taming elephants. Asian elephants accepted being tame (not domesticated) because they enjoyed learning new activities from human companions. According to Juliet Clutton-Brock, senior researcher in the Mammal Section of the Museum of Natural History in London, tamed elephants are exploited captives. Humans have successfully bred horses that, when used in battle, might turn in terror but will obey their owners and not trample soldiers lying on the ground. A domesticated horse will die accepting a command. Elephants in battle never accepted unquestioned human dominance. Clutton-Brock underscores that when trained as war animals, elephants turn dangerous and are unwilling to follow a command. Elephants, when "assailed by a multitude of arrows [will] very sensibly turn around and go backwards, thereby inflicting worse damage" on their own army than on the enemy (Clutton-Brock 1999: 149).

Despite failure in selective breeding for domestication, Indian elephants have had a long relationship with humans as conscripted captives, especially for aiding human war efforts in ancient history. Of the two main types of elephants, the Asian elephant contrasts with African varieties because they bonded with humans over the course of 3,000 years. Prized as war tools by North Indian imperial and regional rulers from 1000 BCE onward, elephants were captured alive in stockades (with the help of a tamed elephant as decoy), with nooses, or in prepared pits. Sometimes adults were killed to capture infants (Clutton-Brock 1999: 148).

The earliest Sanskrit epics, *Ramayana* and *Mahābhārata*, depict elephants as essential components in warfare (as well as in royal and military processions). The second book of the *Mahābhārata* notes that sixty years old is the most suitable age for a war elephant (Indian elephants live for sixty to seventy years) (Singh 1965: 81). The symbolic association of kingship with elephants from the Vedic period onward also made them a sign of prestige diplomacy among potentates (Ottewill-Soulsby 2023). The gift of a live elephant, especially a white one, was a sign of the power and allure of the participants in diplomatic relations in elite Eurasia in the Middle Ages.

Just as the extraction of ivory joined the exploitation of other resources, animals, and peoples (Somerville 2016), so did the extraction of live elephants. The history of captive elephants exploited the humans who worked as elephant drivers, many of whom lived a life of captivity. Taming culture in ancient India centered on the assigned driver, or mahout, which ensured each elephant a human handler. Despite their forced separation from others of their species, tamed elephants formed close bonds with their human handlers. Like certain dogs, some elephants even died of grief when their companion human died.

Recruited into other jobs such as hauling logs, Indian elephants became in-between creatures, no longer part of their kin's world and, often, never fully accepting life as captives.

Like humans, wild elephants are powerful ecosystem engineers that radically alter the landscapes where they live (Somerville 2016: 10–11). With settlement based on agriculture, elephants were eliminated as a threat to the community's food security because they damaged cultivated fields. Elephants needed to consume massive amounts of food long before they grew up and became suitable for battle. Rulers in the Vedic period therefore protected lush forest lands for elephants. As opposed to the destruction of habitats for elephants to clear land for agriculture in many parts of the world, the practice of holding captive elephants for war preserved land for the animals (Trautmann 2015). It also created an economy of elephant care among kings in Southeast Asia.

In contrast to northern Indian regions, the ruling families in China did not make a tradition of using elephants in warfare. In the thirteenth century, China realized the futility of using elephants in war. After Kublai Khan (1215–94), emperor of the Yuan, or Mongol, Dynasty (1271–1368), captured 200 elephants from the Burmese, the Chinese learned that elephants were easily outmaneuvered by any cavalry, were easily frightened, and retreated when confronted with firearms and cannon (Laufer 1925: 18–19). As David Graff, historian of Chinese military history, writes: "The Song dynasty (and earlier times) did not use elephants in warfare. They were too easily frightened, too unpredictable, and if turned against the attackers, created chaos, death, and confusion. While they might have been used by Annamese and others in the jungles of southeast Asia, they never became part of Song military strategy" (Graff 2000, 145).

Even though the Song created stables for their imported elephants, no successful breeding program developed. Supplies were constantly replenished from Vietnam, which included elephants and their mahouts. In captivity in China, the lives of elephants were often filled with torment or spent in a sexless captivity subject to the needs of the state unless, in rare instances, the elephant ended up in a monastery cared for by monks.

The conservation of forest habitats in Southeast Asia for the Asian elephant and the culture of elephant caring developed among Indigenous Southeast Asian peoples were not established in other places where humans recruited elephants for their needs. Although elephant war techniques did not spread to China, they did travel westward after the Macedonian Alexander the Great (356–323 BCE) defeated the Persian king Darius and his cavalry of fifteen elephants (in 331 BCE) and crossed the Indus River into northern India, defeating the Indian king Poros (d. 326 BCE), who set up a line of trained elephants in a defense posture.

The animal became an icon of power and a sign of victory for Alexander. The symbolic significance of the elephant traveled much more easily than the animal. Ancient historians repeated the legend about Alexander and elephants: he captured Poros' elephant, created gold rings for his tusks, and named the animal Ajax. Live Indian elephants took part in Alexander's funeral procession, and images of war elephants were painted on the carriage holding his body (Kistler 2006: 41).

Alexander's successors, the Seleucids, a Greek imperial power in West Asia during the Hellenistic period, continued the tradition of taming Indian elephants for war. The Seleucids made a treaty with Chandrgupta Maurya (350–295 BCE) in which Seleukos Nikator (358–281 BCE) ceded claim to any lands in the Indus Valley in return for 500 war elephants, which he used successfully in the next generation of wars in the lands further west. Seleukos Nikator's Indian elephants had their home base in Syria – Hannibal would later name his favorite elephant Syros, meaning the Syrian (J. McInerney, pers. comm., 2024).

In contrast to India, the custom of preserving forests and mahout bonding never became established for taming elephants in the Mediterranean region. The Ptolemies, a dynasty in Egypt during the Hellenistic period (305–30 BCE), used local Eritrean African elephants. Excavations at Berenike, an ancient Egyptian seaport on the Red Sea, provides powerful evidence of the possible presence of Indian elephant handlers helping to operate the Ptolemaic business (J. McInerney, pers. comm., 2024). The Ptolemies also had limited success with long-term use of the animals in war, and eventually populations of elephants in the Nile Delta were completely exterminated. Nonetheless, scholars cite the battle led by the pharaoh Ptolemy IV (221–204 BCE) at Raphia (217 BCE), often called the Battle of the Elephants, as significant in convincing the Greeks of the value of war elephants (see Polybius 5.84) (J. McInerney, pers. comm., 2024). The Egyptian appetite for ivory was whetted after the elephants were gone. Elephantine, the administrative center for Egyptian-controlled Nubia, received its name because of quantities of ivory sent to the Egyptian capitals from southeast Africa through this trading city (Kistler 2006: 2).

Following the Ptolemies in Egypt, ancient Carthage, home to Hannibal, used tamed elephants for war. In a broad sense, all Mediterranean uses of war elephants descend from the encounter between Alexander and war elephants, but Hannibal used elephants probably in imitation of Pyrrhus of Epirus (319–272 BCE), who campaigned in Italy and Sicily with elephants fifty years before Hannibal. Hannibal's thirty-seven elephants famously crossed Iberia and the Alps in the Punic Wars, to be used as a surprise tactic against the Romans – all the animals except for one died during the winter of 217.

The Carthaginians attempted to house captive elephants. Stables were built to house 300 elephants, and in the early years of the program Indian mahouts were hired and brought to Carthage through Egypt, although in later years riders were brought from Numidia and Egypt (Kistler 2006: 98). Breeding largely failed, and elephants had to be replenished through capture from mountain forests around Carthage in present-day Libya (at Edough and Medjerda). As a last resort in war – and evidence of domestication failure – an order existed for mahouts in Carthage's battles to carry a long spike and hammer. If the animal panicked and turned back on troops, drivers were instructed to attempt to kill the animal by driving the spike into the elephant's neck behind the ear (Kistler 2006: 127).

The Romans largely followed the Carthage model. With elephant populations in Italy extinct, the Romans shipped the animals, probably two per ship, for victory celebrations in special transport vessels (*elephantegoi*) across the Mediterranean (Stevenson 2021: 29; Sidebotham 2019: 49). Romans trained one elephant to walk a tightrope. Others were employed in battles. Some marched with their human drivers celebrating victories, were forced by their handlers to stomp deserters, or were displayed as exotics. By far, most live elephants in ancient Rome were set upon other animals or humans in *venationes* (staged animal hunts) (J. McInerney, pers. comm., 2024). Rome also had to regularly replenish supplies from herds after limited success in keeping an imperial herd in Latium, an area in west central Italy. Aside from noting that the elephants in Latium failed to breed, Juvenal (Decimus Junius Juvenalis, ca. 55–138 CE), a Roman poet, noted that the elephants in Latium refused to carry drivers on their back, an indication that the Romans never developed a mahout culture of elephant–human bonding.

Like the Chinese and the Egyptians, the Carthaginians and Romans not only recruited live elephants but developed an appetite for their ivory. The Romans were largely responsible for the extermination of an entire sub-species of the African elephant (*Loxodonta africana pharaohensis*). The orator Themistius (317–ca. 388) warned that the North African elephant variety would go extinct. His prediction was correct, although premature (Cutler 1985: 2).

The extinct North African or Carthage species of elephant was similar to the two African elephant varieties that still roam in limited areas of sub-Saharan Africa today, which have larger ears in comparison to the Asian elephant. Also, in contrast to the Asian elephant with its convex, upturned back, the North African elephant, like other African elephants, had a dip between its fore and hindquarters, giving its back a concave look, that is, it was curved or rounded downward. At two and a half meters, the North African or Carthage elephant, captured in the Atlas region, was similar in height to contemporary sub-Saharan forest elephants.

Long before ivory was used for the keys of the first pianos in the eighteenth century, human cultures shaped elephant ivory into all kinds of objects that were not only exquisitely fashioned art objects, but also utilitarian. The Carthaginians used ivory from the North African elephant for tablets containing government records, and the Romans expanded ivory use to artificial teeth and pillars to support dining tables. The Roman emperor Caligula built a trough out of ivory for his favorite horse (Cutler 1985: 22–23). As art historian Anthony Cutler underscores in his study of the craft of ivory in the Mediterranean from 200–1400 CE, African elephants were killed at a much faster rate than their tusks grew, making it only a matter of time before ivory grew scarce in one region and new sources were exploited. Asian elephants were also killed at a much faster rate than they could be replenished during the same period. The Song Dynasty not only used African-sourced ivory but also exterminated Asian elephants for ivory for everyday use such as chopsticks, combs, and hairpins. Song government officials typically recorded administrative notes on the back of ivory staves.

From the eighth to the eleventh centuries, the routes that had supplied ivory from elephants from North Africa to Carthage and Rome were supplanted by overland routes and ship routes from Swahili East Africa, such as from the kingdom of the Great Zimbabwe or Zanzibar (Guérin 2022: 9–10; Horton 1996; Shalem 2005a). The tenth-century market for ivory in Europe and beyond was met by the Swahili corridor's increased connection with the Red Sea trade and access to Egyptian markets (Guérin 2022: 10–11; Horton 1996). The East African routes supplied Christian elites in Europe, including Byzantium/ Constantinople and the Saxon dynasty of German monarchs in Ottonian lands in central Europe (919–1024). Ivory from savannah elephants also passed along supply routes from the eastern part of sub-Saharan Africa and was shipped to the Fatimid Caliphate, which from 909 to 1171 included a large swathe of northern Africa, including parts of modern-day Egypt, and to the Cordovan Caliphate, ruled by the Umayyad dynasty on the Iberian Peninsula in Andalusia from 929 to 1031. Ivory from East Africa was also shipped to the Song in China. The Chinese valued African ivory as superior, and one source from Baghdad from the tenth century complained that Chinese markets were draining supplies of African-sourced ivory.

Demand in the Middle Ages pushed the expansion of trade routes further into sub-Saharan Africa. In the case of the West, ivory increasingly arrived from Central and West Africa, especially through the Mediterranean island of Majorca, to supply the heightened demand for Christian icons. In China, particularly the dynasties from the late thirteenth century onward, the Yuan (1279–1368) and the Ming Dynasties (1368–1644), turned ivory into an art. In the fifteenth century, the Chinese expanded global ivory networks to meet its demand. Led by Zheng He (1371–1433), ships returned from Southeast Africa to China with elephant ivory sourced from Africa. Portuguese vessels in the fifteenth century began to source from the West African coast and supplied markets in the Far East. Many of those same vessels also supplied African-sourced ivory to Europe, where it would continue to be carved into luxury objects.

This Element focuses on the significance of ivory especially in the thirteenth century, a period marked by the increased sourcing of ivory from Central and West Africa when it was primarily exported on overland routes across the Sahara. Aside from examining the history of elephants and ivory in China and Spain, we focus on two ivory artifacts: a stave from the Song Dynasty from an Asian elephant and an exquisitely crafted Virgin and Child statuette from Alfonsin Spain from an African elephant. Both objects were crafted in the same century. The focus on the stave highlights that Chinese society was still using ivory for everyday objects when Europe had reached the point of only using ivory for luxury objects.

The Element also focuses on live elephants. Aside from a global desire for ivory that increasingly made it a high-demand item, live elephants were even more of a rare exotic in medieval Europe. While the Chinese were marching Asian elephants and their mahouts to the country from the south, it was nearly impossible to import Asian elephants and their mahouts to the West until the fifteenth century when the Portuguese developed the shipping technology to carry back the live cargo on the nearly 5,000-kilometer journey from Asia to Europe.

The shipping of live Indian, rather than African, elephants, continued well after the early modern period. Jumbo was an exception in the shipping of live African elephants – Indian, not African, elephants supplied newly created zoos and circuses. In an unusual attempt at the exportation of live African elephants in post-Roman times, King Leopold of Belgium became an early pioneer when he sent an African forest elephant to Antwerp Zoo in 1903.

3 Elephants in China

During the Middle Ages, the Chinese imported a steady supply of live elephants. Even though the Song (Northern: 960–1125; Southern: 1125–1279) did not use elephants in warfare, they used them extensively for imperial processions. The Song Dynasty, a cultural zenith in later imperial Chinese history, was partly Buddhist, partly Daoist, but institutionally and ritually Confucian. The Song had become quite aware of how important elephants were as symbols of power in ritual symbology, but they also provided them as spectacle for the large audiences in the densely populated Song capitals. There were more than a million inhabitants in the capital Kaifeng in the north.

The first period of the dynasty, the Northern Song, considered the elephant a potent emblem of the power of the emperor and the state, one to use triennially in the Southern Suburban Sacrifice at the Altar of Heaven, located outside the southern gate of the capital (Figure 2). South is a significant direction, considered the source of the fullness of yang power and the direction that nurtures growth, and it is represented by the color red in the Five Phases. Red symbolizes heat, the power of yang in the yin–yang balance of the cosmos, and above all the life force itself in humans, visible in the ruddy complexion of healthy humans (Figure 3). In a parade to the altar, six or more elephants led the procession of the emperor's entourage from the palace to the sacrificial site. The state sacrificed animals, including goats, pigs, cows, and perhaps horses, to ancestors and sages. The animal sacrifices did not include elephants; however, they were the animal protagonists in processions to the sacrifice.

The elephants formed two lines in front of the Grand Entourage, the most important part of the parade, often comprising 12,000 or more participants from the civil bureaucracy and from the imperial guard, known as the Palace Command. Among a long, forty-volume set of administrative documents of various sorts (mostly petitions, requests, memorials, imperial commands, rescripts, and fiats) categorized according to person, place, event, or thing – *Edited Administrative Documents from the Song* – we can find a series of documents related to the complex system of tribute that brought elephants from Vietnam. From a section on the sumptuary rules for "Carriages and Clothing" we find:

> **Elephants to Lead the Imperial Entourage**
> Flags and implements for the imperial carriage: I: Elephants: In the Han Dynasty (206 BCE to 220 CE) imperial retinue the elephant came first. After Jin had pacified Wu (279–280), Nam Việt sent tame[1] elephants to them as tribute. A large cart was constructed for it/them[2] to pull, to carry several tens of drum and wind players. The Việt person was instructed to ride on the elephant to test bridges.[3]
>
> In the ritual entourages of *our* state, the elephant is placed at the beginning. A wooden lotus flower howdah, a plate topped with golden banana leaves, a purple embroidered covering of silk, and a netting for the head are

---

[1] The Chinese word for "tame" belongs to a word family that means docile and compliant. The same word is used for other animals.

[2] Classical and literary Chinese is a mostly non-inflected language, and a single-syllable pronoun can indicate either singular or plural.

[3] This would be the mahout who accompanied his beast, which according to a record of their captivity, is given a name.

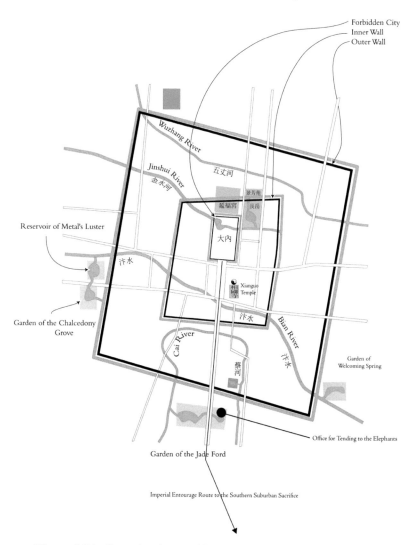

Figure 2 Bianliang (modern Kaifeng). Capital of the Northern Song.
Drawn by Stephen West.

all put on the beast. Bells and apricot leaves of brass are put on the chest and
on the rear cruppers. A red tail sweeps away the dust that it trails. One Nam
Việt soldier rides astride the elephant, and four people – all in long tailed caps
with flowered tails, narrow doublets of crimson embroidery, and silver belts –
lead the elephants. (Xu Song 2008: *yufu*.3.15)

How the elephant came to be so important has to do with the unbidden arrival
of elephants (both tame and rogue) at the capital in Bianliang (modern Kaifeng)
in the earliest years of the Song. On one occasion, an elephant suddenly appeared

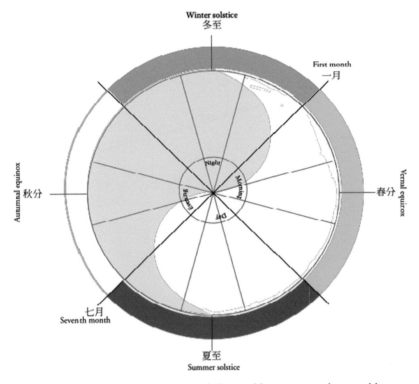

Figure 3 Chart of yin and yang correlations with seasons, colors, and hours. Springs begin on the third dark moon after the winter solstice. All annual ritual activities are coded as belonging to a certain season of the year. The Southern Suburban Sacrifice occurs on or near the advent of the first lunar month. Drawn by Stephen West.

on its own: "On the day *yisi* in the third lunar month of the first year of the Kaibao reign (April 2, 968) a tame elephant reached the capital by itself. All the officials celebrated it by memorial" (Li Tao 1985: 201). Such a propitious appearance by an elephant has a long history in the symbology of auspicious events and was believed to have been brought about in response to the ethical power of the emperor. There are several such events recorded in history,[4] most of which employ the ancient phrase, "when the ruler is self-regulated [in his consumption], an elephant will arrive on its own" (Shen Yue et al. 2018: vol. 2, 802 and Wei Shou et al. 2017: vol. 8, 2928). The source of this quote can be traced back to the earliest commentaries on the *Classic of Change* (*Yijing*), where it is discussed in an early interpretation of the hexagram "nourishment" (*yi* 頤): "Augured as

---

[4] The most famous being one in 538, which caused a change in reign title in the Eastern Wei. See Wei Shou et al. 2017.

correct, therefore propitious. Observe nourishment and what one seeks to place in the mouth." In a major Song Dynasty commentary by Zhu Xi 朱熹 (1130–1200), it is understood as follows: "The mouth consumes things to keep one alive, and it nurtures righteousness" (Zhu Xi 1992: 38). That is, this method of perfecting one's own body and being through self-regulation of intake forms the basis for understanding the concept of regulation in the nourishment of all phenomena, including the Way of Heaven.

One important result of the appearance of this elephant was the establishment of the Office for Tending to Elephants (*Yangxiang suo* 養象所), which institutionalized the care and feeding of these tribute gifts. As recorded in the *History of the Song*, the emperor was quick to establish a permanent location in the Garden of the Jade Ford (*Yujin yuan* 玉津園) south of the city (see Figure 2): "In the eighth lunar month of the fifth year of Qiande reign (September–October), an elephant came from the south on its own, and had been around the capital for ten days or more. [Officials] commanded the 500 soldiers from Xuzhou and the Fenghua Borough Army to seize it, and he established the Office for Tending to Elephants" (Xu Song 2008: *zhiguan*.23.3; Toqto et al. 1985: vol. 11, 4644). The office, along with others involved with animals and conveyances, was assigned to the Court for Conveyances and Animals (*Taipu si* 太僕寺).[5] From this time onward, elephants were quartered in the garden in the winter and spring months and sent away to pasture in an area about seventy-two miles east-south-east of Kaifeng in early summer:

> The Office for Tending to Elephants was located in the northeast of the Garden of the Jade Ford and was in charge of the care and feeding of tame elephants. Every fourth lunar month they would send the elephants to pasture along the northern banks of the Bian River, west of Ningling District in Yingtian Superior Prefecture. In the ninth month, they would return. Annually, the Garden of the Jade Ford would be ordered to broadcast wild rice seeds for elephant food [i. e., the stalks and awns] over fifteen *qing* (±247 acres). (Xu Song 2008: *zhiguan*.23.3)

It was in Ningling that the Japanese monk Jōjin 成尋 (1011–81) and his entourage had a chance to visit the elephants in their stables and were given a grand tour:

> On the seventh day, *shinshi* (November 18, 1072), the sky was clear. In the first twenty-four-minute period of the double hour of the rabbit (5:00–5:24 a.m.), we

---

[5] This included the Cart and Wagon Service, Service for Distant Travel, the Left and Right Equine Stables, Left and Right Directorates for Warhorses, Left and Right Directorates of Fine Steeds, Higher and Lower Directorates of Veterinary Services, Storehouse for Saddles and Tack, Camel Paddocks, Office of Skinning, and Court for Imperial Conveyances. See Toqto et al. 1985: vol. 14, 4691.

set out on the boat. By the double hour of the snake (9:00–11:00 a.m.) we had reached the government offices of Song Prefecture. There was a large bridge, and at the side of the river was the Ningling District Hostel. We immediately passed it by for one *li* (about 0.5 of a kilometer) and then moored the boat.

I then mounted the palanquin of the Military Escort Official, and after traveling for about a *chō* and a half (165 meters) we reached the elephant stables. One building held three elephants and one building held four. We first visited the three elephants. The person who fed the elephants instructed the elephant that, because a foreign monk and his party had come, he could make obeisance. The first elephant bent its two rear legs and crouched with its head lowered. Next, being instructed that it could make a formal greeting, it immediately trumpeted by expelling air. The elephant was one *jō* and three *shaku* tall (almost four meters), one *jō* and six *shaku* long (4.85 meters); its nose was more than six *shaku* long (1.81 meters), and its tusk was seven *shaku* long (2.12 meters) and curved upward. It grasped fodder by curling its nose around it to eat it. We gave the mahout 50 cash.

Then we went off toward the second elephant stall, where the mahout also begged for some cash, and we gave him five [fifty?] cash. [The elephant] made obeisance and a formal greeting as before. It was one *jō* high (3 meters), one *jō* and three *shaku* (3.94 meters) in length, and it had tusks. Then we went to the third elephant stall, and the elephant was similar in height and length to the first, it also made obeisance and trumpeted a formal greeting as before, and we gave the same amount of money as before. All of these three elephants were male.

We reached the stable of the four elephants. The first elephant was the same size as the one before. The first elephant trumpeted a formal greeting, and we gave money just as before. It was a female elephant. It had a left tusk, one *shaku* and a half in length (0.45 meters) but was missing a right tusk. The second elephant was a female without tusks. The oral greeting and cash given was the same as before. The third elephant was a breeding male. It was one *jō* and three *shaku* tall (3.92 meters), one *jō* and four *shaku* in length (4.24 meters), and it knelt on all four legs to trumpet its greeting – an extremely loud sound that startled everyone. Three sounds came out, and we gave money as before. The fourth elephant was also a breeding male. We gave five cash.

Later the mahout mounted the elephant using its tusk. It was a rare thing, indeed, to see a tusk raised to let a person mount the head. It was more than one *jō* and four *shaku* tall (4.24 meters), and more than one *jō* and eight *shaku* (6.09 meters) in length. It knelt on its back legs and trumpeted its greeting as before. All of the elephants are black. The back two legs are fettered by a rope. There was fodder stacked everywhere like mountains, and each elephant is fed fifteen *jin* a day; the stalks of the feed are more than eight *shaku* (2.42 meters) long. Elephants were originally kept in cities by the King of Guangnan[6] for warfare, and after [the Song] had broken the Guangnan area, they began to be raised here, so it is said. The elephants have no hair, and

---

[6] A reference to the Southern Han dynasty (917–71), which was defeated by the Song. Originally comprised of the areas of Guangdong, Guangxi, Hainan Island, Hong Kong and Macau, and a portion of Vietnam (later lost), with its capital at modern Guangzhou (Canton).

their skin looks like that of the black cows of Japan, which turn a dark grey color when their hair drops. The sheath and the shape of their penises are both like those of a horse, and the nipples of the female elephants are like those of a pig. Today we traveled forty-eight *li* (27.35 kilometers). (Jōjin 2009, 267–268; following the notes of Fujiyoshi in Jōjin 2007, 395–397)

There were precise stipulations about how these elephants should be decorated on their journey when they returned to the capital from the pastureland:

> In the seventh lunar month of the sixth year of Xining reign of Emperor Shenzong (August 6–September 4, 1073), the *Stipulations for Training the Elephants for the Southern Sacrifice* was promulgated. There were to be seven elephants.[7] An imperial directive was sent down to Ningling District in Yingtian Superior Prefecture about sending the elephants to the capital on the first day of the ninth month.
>
> To be used [as panoply] on this trip: Fifteen flags from the Court of Imperial Sacrifice, one bronze washpan gong,[8] ten cylinder-drums; seven mahout and thirty-one people in a cluster to lead the musicians. When assembling the entourage, select six elephants from these seven to be put in front of the entourage; they are to march in the middle of the road, divided to the left and right. Each is to be equipped with a saddle, decorated seat, a saddle cushion of purple embroidered silk, a flat dish of banana leaves (i.e., a plate comprised of banana leaf replicas placed around a radiating perimeter), locked belts, apricot leaves, and a net for the head. It is to be ridden by one person, surrounded by four others, and all shall wear black scarves with decorated tails, crimson robes, four-slit over-robes embroidered with green cherries and sewed together (at the top?) with tassels, and double-deer belts daubed with gold. One person from the Inner [Eunuch] Servants will lead the elephants, holding a long club and wearing embroidery. (Xu Song 2008: *zhiguan*.23.9–10)

These elephants rehearsed the long parade route from the Palace to the sacrifice site (Figure 3.3). An eyewitness account for the years 1103–26 gives a brief account of the rehearsal:

> In years when there is the major ritual [of Sacrifice to Heaven], about two months ahead of time, the carriages and elephants [to be used in the imperial procession] are instructed through rehearsal. They make a round-trip circuit from the Gate of Virtue Displayed out beyond the Gate of Southern Infusion.
>
> There are five carriages: these are used to stand in for the five imperial carriages.[9] There are two flags and one drum installed on each carriage, which

---

[7] That is, six for the parade and one extra, should one of the elephants get sick or surly.

[8] These were shallow bowls, used primarily in the military as gongs for announcing particular times; at other times, they were used as washbasins.

[9] These are conveyances adorned with jade, gold, ivory, hide, or wood on the ends of the pieces of the cart that show; there is a stipulated ridership for the carts, from the emperor down through the hierarchy of family and bureaucrats.

Figure 4 An anonymous artist's portrayal of a procession of elephants being trained as well as practice carts pulled by four-horse teams in front of the Gate of Virtue. Detail of an imitation of "Riverside Scene at Qingming Festival" by Song Dynasty painter Zhang Zeduan (1085–1145). Undated. Unknown provenance. Public domain.

is pulled by a four-horse team. The imperial guards that are in file on either side of the carriages are dressed in hats and purple robes. There are several people in front of the carriages to crack whips.

Seven head of elephants: several tens of vermilion flags are arranged in ranks in front of them, along with several tens of bronze gongs and several tens of drums large and small. First the gongs are struck twice, and the drums quickly respond with three beats. The flag bearers are robed in purple and wear hats. One person, dressed in a cross-tailed cloth hat and robed in purple, straddles the neck of each elephant. He holds a short-handled bronze billhook that has been tapered to a point. If the elephant is not compliant, he strikes it. When the elephants reach the Gate of Virtue Displayed, they circle around a few times before forming ranks. They are made to face north and kneel, and they can also trumpet on command.

All of the maternal relatives and in-laws [of the emperor], members of the royal family, and families of nobility summon the elephants to their private residence where they can look at them closely, and there is no day in which [the mahout] are not given silver and colored silks.

The roamers on the Imperial Avenue gather happily together, and the observers seem as though tightly woven together. They gamble for little elephants fashioned from clay, wood, or dough as well as paper cutouts. The onlookers carry these items home in order to present them to others. (Meng Yuanlao 1999: vol. 3, 883–888)

Moreover, since the Chinese graph denoting elephant (象) was very early on adapted to also mean "image," "sign," or "symbol," the elephant's appearance from the south was a concrete presence of a propitious sign of the eventual capitulation of lands lying along the southern perimeter to the armies of the Song. This area was also the origin of most tame elephants. The sudden appearance of the beast in the capital Bianliang in 968 gave the elephant its place as a symbol of royal prestige and power in the consciousness of the people, and elephants were conspicuously on display as part of the many imperial retinues to sacrificial sites during the year. A look at the central axial Imperial Avenue that ran from the palace to the sacrificial sites south of the city, traversed by a triennial parade of some 12,500 officials or more, shows clearly how this entourage, which was ritual for the court, was more of a spectacle for citizens of the capital (cf. Ebrey 1999).

In the fourth year of the founding of the Song (963), there had been a tribute of rare items sent to court: a yellow parrot, a white rabbit, and a tame elephant. To mark this occasion, three flags were created (among many others) to be carried in the Southern Suburban entourage.[10] A further embedding of tame elephants into rituals occurred a few years later, when the Assistant Minister of the Court of Imperial Sacrifice suggested that the elephants be incorporated into sacrificial hymns to be used at all sacrifices.

---

[10] "In the fourth year of the Jianlong reign, there were tributes of a yellow parrot, a white hare, and a tame elephant; from this point forward, they created flags of the golden parrot and others [to be used in the entourage]" (Toqto et al. 1985: vol. 10, 3400).

On Qiande 6.10.27 reign (20 November 986) He Xian (933–88) made a recommendation, "When the Han Dynasty obtained the heavenly horses, the red crane, and the white unicorn (an albino rhinoceros), for each they created a song to be sung at the Suburban Sacrifices. Our state has received an auspicious piece of wood in the shape of characters reading 'the great continuous Song,' a tame elephant has come from the southern quadrant on its own, a white horse was captured in Qinzhou, and a white (albino?) sparrow: all of these should be broadcast through pipes and strings and offered up at the Sacrifices to Heaven, Earth and Ancestors. The emperor ordered Xian to create four auspicious songs, 'Auspicious Text,' 'Tame Elephant,' 'Jade Corvidae,' and 'Hoary Sparrow' to be sung at sacrifice." (Ouyang Xiu et al. 2002: 27.2a, 456)

The elephant then assumed the lead position in the imperial entourage parade to the Southern Sacrifice, a total of six equally divided on the left and right. The Song also began the practice of placing stone elephants on the approaches, called "spirit ways," to the tumuli of emperors, where sacrificial ceremonies were held to commemorate former rulers. This practice continued until the Qing Dynasty (1644–1911), a common and familiar sight until that time for visitors to the Song and Ming imperial tombs. Thus, in the years 907–1125, the elephant was not only associated with the emperor, but it was also deeply embedded in the minds of the subjects of the Song as a concrete manifestation of imperial power. One must also concede, however, that the onlookers in the Northern Song capital (as shown in the previously cited passage) could also be more attracted to the spectacle of the entourage and its rehearsal than by its overt use as an imperial symbol, while the spectacle itself also carries with it all the while an acknowledgment of the power behind it.

When the northern capital of the Song was sacked in the year 1125 by the Jurchen Jin dynasty (1115–1234), one of the imperial sons fled, and he made several attempts, constantly under pressure from Jurchen campaigns, to find a place to resurrect the court and the dynasty (see the peripatetic seats of government in Notes about the Text). While it took some time to reestablish the state, the Gaozong emperor 高宗 (1107–87, r. 1127–62), who reigned for thirty-six years before abdicating, took pains to adopt the institutions and ritual forms of the founding emperor of the Song and was eager as well to keep elephants visible as material symbols of the dynasty's continuity. He reigned, according to Chinese sources, from 1127–62, when he retired. He moved around but eventually settled on Hangzhou as his capital in 1131.

Elephants were often captured somewhere in the forests south-southeast of modern Hanoi, on Mount Lương. As described in a late twelfth-century geo-ethnography by Zhou Qufei 周去非 (1135–89), the capture and training of elephants was exceptionally cruel:[11]

> In the mountains of Jiaozhi are natural stone enclosures, with only one path of ingress and encircled by rock walls. People of Jiao first place fodder there and then drive a tame female elephant into it. Then they spread sugar cane on the road to attract wild elephants. Waiting until they are enticed to eat the cane, they then release the tame female into the herd, and entice her to return to the enclosure. Once they have all entered, the passageway into the enclosure is blocked by a large boulder.
>
> Only after the wild elephants get very hungry does a person traipse around the top of the rock wall to feed them. The wild elephants, although trepidatious in the beginning, will see the female being fed and in the end, they will also cozy up to get food. As they become more familiar, a person thrashes them with a stick and, as they become a bit tamer, one can ride them and control them.
>
> In most cases, to control an elephant, one must use a billhook. When a person from Jiao tames an elephant, they sit directly astride its neck and hold the iron billhook in their hand to gouge the head of the elephant. If the rider wants the elephant to go left, he gouges the right side of the head; if right is desired, he strikes the left; to make it walk backwards, he gouges its forehead, if he wants the elephant to go forward, then there is no hook applied. Should he desire the elephant to kneel in prostration, he gouges the hook straight down on the top of the head and then pushes down a second time more heavily. The elephant trumpets in pain and people, seeing it do so, think that the beast is making a formal greeting. When people see them forming into ranks in a herd or walking in an evenly spaced line, they do not understand that it is only by virtue of the billhook that the elephant goes forward, backs up, or moves to the left and right.
>
> As an animal, even though it is large, it cannot stand pain, so a person can make it docile with a few inches of the hook. By and by the elephant understands what the person [i.e., his mahout] means, and seeing the elephant rider approaching, it will bow its head and kneel down in front; when the person gets on its neck, the elephant rouses up and begins to take off.
>
> An elephant cannot bend its head to look down, and the neck cannot turn sideways. Its mouth is sunken away into its cheeks and is a long way away from the ground. All activities of eating and drinking are done through the use of his trunk. The end of the trunk is large and deep, and [its nostrils] can be opened and closed. In the middle is a small fleshy pincer [the Asian elephant's

---

[11] The capture of pachyderms was quite a bit different in Tajik (大食), an area of modern Iraq and the Arabian Peninsula. In a late eleventh-century set of notes, we read, "In my duties I was in charge of *The Record of Tribute*, and in the *zhidao* reign period (995–8), Man Ximi (likely a mistranscription of Pu Ximi 蒲希密, Abu Hamid) of the Tajik state sent a male with tribute, who said that his state produced only rhinoceroses and elephants. A rescript inquired how they were taken, and he replied that an elephant go-between (tame female) would entice others which were gradually tied up with ropes. Rhinoceros were taken by an archer lying in wait under a large tree. He would wait until one would arrive and then kill it with arrows. No bow and arrows were needed for small ones, which could also be lassoed" (Pang Yuanying 2006: 123).

single prehensile digit] that can pick up even a tiny mustard seed. Whenever it takes food to eat with its trunk, it first uses its foot and phalanges to smash it and get out the dirt and mud; only then does it take the food to curl it to put into its mouth. In drinking water, it also sucks it up and curls its trunk to deposit it in the mouth. When the new liquor made by people in small villages matures, wild elephants track its fragrance down, smash through the walls with their trunks, come in, and drink it – this is a great anxiety for people.

The legs of an elephant are like posts, they have no digits but only hardened nails on their feet. In going up high mountains, down steep slopes, or crossing the water despite its ponderous form, it is extremely nimble. The people of Jiao summon it to ride, and it seems they can actually communicate with it. Sent on tribute missions, a single elephant will not remain tame and will quickly perish. It will moan and groan for a few days and just before it passes away, it will turn its head to the south to die. This ability to "face its head towards its den" when it dies shows that the elephant is no ordinary animal. There are also some in the areas around Qinzhou.

An elephant will always travel on a familiar path. People sometimes embed a mechanism with blades on a wooden structure on the side of the path that is anchored to the ground. When the elephant triggers it as it walks, the blades come down from above and strike its body. Should they strike right on a crucial point and severely injure the elephant, it will certainly die. As it is about to die, it will break its tusks off on a boulder, as if understanding that it was the tusks themselves that brought such disaster to its body. If it is not a severe injury then it will walk off with the knives still in it, and when its flesh festers the blades simply fall out. Those otherwise not severely injured but whose trunks are harmed will also die. Since it uses its trunk for every single daily activity, once it is cut there is no way to rejoin it.[12] The very thing that gives it such ability brings it death.

Some use pitfalls to kill elephants. About a dozen feet from the side of the elephant's accustomed path, they work the earth at an angle [to undercut the path] and make a pitfall. They restore the appearance of the road; the elephant, suspecting nothing, treads on it and falls into the pit. So, the old adage "that elephants know whether the ground is firm or not" is just not true. Just make sure there is no loose earth where it will pass.

The eyes of an elephant are tiny, and it is afraid of fire. Wherever elephants gather, they will injure crops. If people are frantic because they cannot control them, they tie fire onto a long pole and chase them until they withdraw. Elephants can harm people: even the largest herds of elephants are not worth fearing. The only thing to be afraid of is a single elephant. Banished from the herd, it travels alone and fears nothing. And, if it encounters someone, it will exercise its poisonous nature, curl the person up in its trunk, hurl him to the ground to kill him, then trample him until blood oozes out of his muscle and flesh. At that point the elephant uses its trunk to drink the human's blood.

---

[12] Fan Chengda clarifies that a cut will not close on the trunk because of its constant activity (Fan Chengda 1781: 7a).

A multitude of people can eat their fill from the meat of a single slaughtered elephant. The trunk is certainly the finest meat. Cook it until tender and put into a mound of wine lees, slice it, and let it ferment.[13] This is one wonder among food items. Elephant hide can be made into shields, for it is exceedingly sturdy. Some people cut its hide into strips, hang it straight with weights at the bottom and dry it, then fashion it into a walking stick that is exceedingly sturdy and fine. (Zhou Qufei 1999: 345–346; cf. Fan Chengda 2010: 69–72)

After elephants had endured such a period of training, they could be chosen to be sent as tribute to the Song state, where they would be further trained to take part in the ritual parades and sacrifices such as the triennial sacrifice to Heaven, held at the Altar of Heaven south of the capital cities of Kaifeng in the north (960–1125) and Hangzhou in the south (1138–1276).

Despite the trouble in establishing a capital, the first emperor of the Southern Song, known as Gaozong, reigned for thirty-two years, from early 1131 to his abdication on the fourth of February in 1163, and his son, known as Xiaozong, reigned for another twenty-seven years, giving the early part of the dynasty a great deal of stability. Tribute convoys were not always allowed to go all the way to the capital. During Gaozong's reign, they were stopped at the border in 1138, 1144, and 1147. Annam sent ten elephants to the capital in March of 1150, but there is no record of a convoy. There were other tribute missions that turned back as well, including those bringing elephants. Convoys were neither easy to arrange nor cost-effective. In Zhou Qufei's work, he remarks on the tribute missions:

> When their state [Annam] sends tribute, they have traditionally entered our borders through Yong or Qin Prefectures (Figure 5). Generally, they first send Head Envoys to clarify and stipulate [conditions under which the trip would be possible], then send a document [a *yiwen* 移文, a document stipulated only for use between non-affiliated offices] to the Military Commissioner [for the respective circuit], which was subsequently sent on to be heard by the emperor. If an imperial order allows the mission to come [to the capital], then a special envoy is dispatched to the capital. If there is no permission, then it does not happen. (Zhou Qufei 1999: 58)

We can see that the planning and execution of such tribute missions took some time. The persons in charge of the convoy would first obtain permission to cross the borders, then permission to visit the Military Commissioner's office in

---

[13] Fan Chengda: "Kill a single elephant and the entire population of a village can have their fill. Its trunk is most delicious. Cook it and cover with wine lees; when they have soaked clear through, cut it into pieces to eat" (Fan Chengda 1781: 7a). In Fan's work, the character *luán* 臠, "to cut into chunks or slices," is used instead of the character *fǔ* 腐, which means "to rot" or "to get soft." Fan's version seems preferable.

Figure 5 First leg of the tribute missions from Annam to the Song capitals, from the border to modern Guilin. Drawn by Stephen West.

Jingjiang (modern Guilin). If he had not been ordered to turn down the, a special envoy would be sent to finalize things in Lin'an (modern Hangzhou), and the tribute mission would be sent upon that envoy's return.

All of the elephants in ceremonies in both the Northern and Southern capitals of the Song were tribute animals. There were generally two types of tribute convoys: normal convoys to replenish the stock of elephants for use in state rituals, and celebratory missions. From the scant evidence we have left, we find normal convoys had groups of either five or ten elephants, while the celebratory missions could have any number (Li Xinchuan 1936: 155.2509; 161.2606). As soon as it was learned that the Southern Song had begun carrying out state rituals in their provisional capitals, a clear indication of a reestablished dynasty in the south, Annam was eager to send regional tributes:

On Jianyan 4.12.2 (January 2, 1131) the Military Commander of the Western Route of Guangnan announced, "The Protectorate of Annam has requested, 'Now preparations are being made for the convoy of regional goods, and we request to go to the capital to present them this autumn.'" An edict:

> Order concerned offices to advise them that, since the border issues have yet to be settled, we are not allowing envoys to go to the capital. As for the regional goods they want to send as tribute, except for luxury goods, which we will not accept, exchange the rest at the border area, and then send guards [from your headquarters] to accompany these items to the Provisional Capital. As for what we grant in return, order the Fiscal and Judicial Commissioners to take funds to disperse from monies in their control, calculate what the standard sum should be, and gift them accordingly in return. Still prepare a list of items and send it by fast messenger along with pertinent memorials. We will await its arrival and then have the Court of Academicians send down a decree to thank them. (Xu Song 2008: *fanyi*.4.42; cf. Li Xinchuan 1936, 40.743)

Annam was the major supplier of tame elephants, and from their perspective, as a state in a position of dependency on the Song for military protection and trade, it was important they keep themselves visible to Song rulers. Special tribute missions were proposed when there were celebratory events: deaths, ascensions to thrones, the completion of peace treaties, for instance. As an example, we should consider requests sent when a king of the Lý kingdom (Nhà Lý, founded in the early eleventh century) in Vietnam passed away and a son inherited his throne. A putative "posthumous memorial" (遺表) would always be sent from the deceased king, and a request to send a convoy was always made, clearly a ploy to solicit favor for the new ruler of Annam. If we consider the magnificent gifts that the Song sent to Annam upon a new king's ascension to throne, it is hard not see the request for a convoy as self-serving – particularly given that they often returned with goods of greater value than they had sent. These convoys were often rebuffed, as in the case of the death of Lý Dương Hoán (李陽煥 r. 1127–38):

> On Shaoxing 8.3.2 (April 12, 1138), an edict:
>
> As for Annam sending in tribute, order the Military Commission of the Western Route of Guangnan to explain that we are not allowing envoys to go to the capital. In the case of all convoys, we will take no luxury goods; as for the rest of the goods, order them to be turned over at the border, and then send them with accompanying guards to the Provisional Capital. In exchange of goods[14] order the Fiscal and Judicial Offices of that Route to take funds out of money under their control and bestow it on them according to precedent.

---

[14] He uses a verb meaning to gift something as an emperor to someone in an inferior position.

Send Zhu Fei 朱芾[Vice-Minister of the Tax Transport Bureau] as Envoy for the Memorial Service to bestow on them 165-meter-long pieces each of silk and cotton, 50 head of goats, 50 *dan* (3,165 kilograms) of flour, 50 vases of wine, 50 bundles of paper, 50 stands of funeral cash, 50 bundles of funeral colored paper, 50 ingots of funeral gold and funeral silver,[15] and order the Fiscal Office to respond with this. The memorials and list of convoy goods can be accepted and sent on with fast messenger. We will wait until it arrives, and then ask the Court of Academicians to write a further rescript to instruct Thiên Tộ.

This rescript resulted from an opinion sent from the Military Commission of the Western Route of Guangxi which said, "The King of Jiaozhi Prefecture Lý Dương Hoán *has passed away. His son,* Thiên Tộ (李天祚, r. 1138–75) will inherit his position. An envoy will go to the capital to present a posthumous memorial from Lý Dương Hoán and a convoy of goods." Therefore, this order was sent. (Xu Song 2008: *fanzhi*.4.42–43)

There was a general resistance to anything but normal tribute. In 1155, Gaozong rebuffed a tribute mission from Champa, saying simply, "In our ancestor's time they used these for the Great Ritual. But we now have tame elephants. If they have not reached the borders, then they can wait there" (Li Xinchuan 1936: 169.2759). But the next year, he allowed two large convoys from Annam to come to Lin'an. It is unclear why he changed his mind, but an account of 1155 gives us some idea:

Shaosing 25.6.*xinmao* (July 16, 1155). The emperor spoke, "After Yang Zaixing [head of the Wuxing Man people] was captured, the various tribes of the Hu and Guang areas [in the south] have all been quiet. This was the effect of simultaneously applying power and grace." [Prime Minister] Qin Hui 秦檜 (1091–1155) said, "Now everyone outside of our four borders all desire to send tribute. Since they come from afar, we should settle them with our virtue." "True," said the emperor. (Li Xinchuan 1936: 168.2753)

Annam seized on the opportunity to couple their regular, normal tribute mission with one that celebrated "ascendent peace," unaware that the Song was still fighting a northern war with the Jin. According to Zhou Qufei's account:

Under the old rules, the Annam group of envoys is superior to that from Gaoli. After the Southern Crossing in the Jianyan reign (1127–30), Lý Thiên Tộ sought to enter tribute.[16] The [Song] court praised his sincerity and responded to him with an especially favorable rescript.

---

[15] To be burned in offering.
[16] This is incorrect: Lý Thiên Tộ 李天祚 (1136–75) was installed on the throne upon his father's death when he was a mere two years old. He reigned from 1138–75, and therefore it is unlikely that he sent such a request. The request was likely made by his father.

The request was answered politely, but the mission was rebuffed by emperor Gaozong:

> 4.12.2 of the Jianyan reign (January 2, 1131) The Military Commissioner of the Western Route of Guangxi announced, "The Protectorate of Annam has requested, 'Now preparations are being made for the convoy of regional goods, and they request to come to the capital to present them this autumn.'" The emperor sent an edict to order concerned offices to advise them that, since the border issues have yet to reach a settled state, we are not allowing envoys to go to the capital. As for the regional goods they want to give as tribute, except for those luxury goods, which we will not accept, exchange them at the border area, and then send a guard to accompany them on the trip to the Provisional Capital. As for what we grant to them, order the Fiscal and Judicial Commissioners to take funds from monies in their control to disperse, calculate what the standard sum should be, and gift them with this in return. Still prepare a list of items and send it by fast messenger along with pertinent memorials. We will await its arrival and then have the Court of Academicians send down a decree to thank them. (Xu Song 2008: *fanyi*. 4.42)

Zhou Qufei continues with his account:

> In the twenty-sixth year of Shaoxing reign (1156–7), a request to enter tribute was made again and it was allowed. Lý sent envoys through the border at Qin. The Head Envoy was Martial Grandee of the Right of Annam, Lý Nghî; the Vice-Envoy was Esquire of the Martial Wings of Annam, Quách Ứng.
> In addition to filling normal quota in the entry convoy of five elephants, they also had a convoy to celebrate ascendant peace (the ascension of a new Southern Song emperor Xiaozong to the throne), and for that convoy the Magistrate of Tháibắng Province of Annam, Lý Quốt, was appointed as head envoy. The objects from their region that they offered in tribute were abundant, and the memorial they presented was written with golden characters. They sent more than 1,200 *liang* (±47 kilograms) of gold objects, half of which were also adorned with gems. They also offered pearls, the three largest being the size of an eggplant,[17] the next six were the size of seeds of the jackfruit, the next twenty-four were the size of peach pits, the next seventeen the size of plum seeds, and the next fifty the size of jujube pits. One hundred all together, they were packed in a golden vase.
> They moreover sent as tribute 1,000 *jin* (±629 kilograms) of aloeswood incense, 50 kingfisher feathers, 850 pieces of dark yellow silk decorated with coiling dragons, 6 imperial mounts, along with saddle and tack, as well as the usual 8 horses and 5 tame elephants. There were fifty underlings for each of the two convoys, and the Head Envoys were self-congratulatory about the abundance of what they had offered in tribute. Later, when they again

---

[17] Probably referring to the Indian or Thai variety of eggplant; the smaller Thai white variety is the source of the general name "eggplant."

requested to enter the border to offer tribute, the court immediately turned
them back. (Zhou Qufei 1999: 59)

From this passage, we observe an interesting moment at the end when the envoys
engaged in self-congratulation (自矜), a display in the face of the hosts of the
mission which is far beyond the bounds of what the Song would have thought
appropriate. This reveals a theme that appears throughout the documents associated with elephant tribute, about the cultural inferiority and crudeness of the
Annamese in Chinese eyes (cf. Whitmore 1986). One can see the extent of disdain
in a cautionary edict promulgated when they envoys returned:

> On Shaoxing 26.9.6 (July 10, 1155) it was decreed, "On the return trip of the
> Annam envoys, they are to be escorted by the original convoy guards who
> accompanied them here. Moreover, have the Transport officials along the
> borders notify each prefecture and military district that they are to be treated
> the same as they were on the trip here. There is to be no ill-treatment nor any
> derisive language." (Xu Song 2008: *fanyi*.4.47)

The Song was beset by problems in the next ten years, among them a renewal of
warfare with the Jin and Gaozong's lack of effectiveness in military strategy,
including removing his most successful generals from their posts. His abdication in 1163 may, it has been suggested, have been the result of ineffectual
management of the wars (Tao 2009: 705–709). Among Gaozong's rescripts, one
in particular stands out:

> In Shaoxing 31.1.6 (February 2, 1161) Annam sent ten tame elephants. On
> this day a grand minister presented the following: "Annam has presented
> tame elephants, order the Commissioner in Guangxi to gift in return." The
> emperor said, "It is the duty of the Man and Yi [barbarians][18] to provide local
> tribute items. But I do not want to give distant people work because of some
> rare beast, nor desire that this beast lose its geo-nature. Order the Route
> Pacification Commissioners to carefully instruct them that from now on,
> normal convoys of tribute do not need to include elephants." (Xu Song
> 2008: *fanyi*.47.7)

The concept of "geo-nature (*tuxing* 土性)" or, as sometimes understood, "geo-
life (*tusheng* 土生)" reflects one of the basic concepts of geomancy. The term
occurs in pre-Han texts in the phrase "one does not raise an animal outside of its
geo-natural range 犬馬非其土性不畜" (Li Min and Wang Jian 2004, 233). It
implies a link between the forces circulating under the earth as a form of

---

[18] The Chinese regularly refer to Man (southern), Yi (eastern), and other peoples less cultured as
"barbarians." Southern Man people were mostly Australo-Asiatic; Yi were predecessors of the
Chinese in eastern China; Hu were mostly Altaic or Tungusic (Turkish, Khitan, Jurchen, and
Manchu).

potential and on top of it as weather patterns, topography, and the nature of living things produced there. The original term for "custom" in modern Chinese, literally "wind-habits" (*fengsu* 風俗), meant behavioral patterns produced locally by a specific combination of both visible and unseen geological and topological forces on the surface and underneath the earth. Animals outside of this comfort zone would suffer because all natural forces are different, as are human attitudes toward them (cf. Lewis 2003).

When the emperor Xiaozong, Gaozong's adopted son, took the throne, it provided a more favorable moment for the people of Annam to send tribute. A new emperor was enthroned, peace had been struck on the northern borders of the Song, and as such another celebratory mission was called for. It also happened to coincide with the moment that the number of tame elephants available for use in imperial rituals had dwindled sharply because of the lack of normal convoys.

Requests were issued that ordered elephants to the capital. One late twelfth-century order included a shipment of ivory and also ten male elephants, on one of which we base the life story of the elephant we call Y Khun. In July 1172, the Camel Paddock, responsible for oversight of the Elephant Compound, sent in a request:

> "Now we are in charge of two tame bull elephants, both of which have exceptionally large teeth. We fear that something might go wrong that would ruin our contribution to the Great Ritual. We request that you order the Military Commission of the Western Route of Guangnan to make plans to gather in ten head of very tame male elephants with young teeth and fine tusks, with a deadline of reaching here before the Great Ritual." This was followed. (Xu Song 2008: *fangyu*.3.49)

The Military Commissioner, so ordered, wanted to purchase elephants from Annam, but their king, Lý Thiên Tộ, took advantage of this to request to send the elephants as part of a celebratory tribute mission. As Fan Chengda, then Commissioner, reported,

> Qiandao 9.6.11 (July 22, 1173), the Office of the Military Commissioner of the Western Route of Guangnan opines, "Recently we ordered Annam to purchase and send ten tame elephants. I have looked at their communication and see that they want to go to the court to provide tribute for the Grand Ritual." A rescript: "According to the directive already sent down on 5.7 (June 18, 1173), wait until the people responsible for leading the elephants arrive, set up the appropriate ritual, and then send them back."
>
> Before this, the court had a directive to purchase bull elephants to provide for the Grand Ritual, but Annam requested by memorial to send tribute. There was an order to accept one of every ten items of things sent. The Prefect of Yong and the Military Commissioner of Guangxi worried that they had erred

in purchasing the elephants, and wanted to wait until there was firm news of their purchase. They had barely sent a report when a herd of the elephants arrived and were accepted. A rescript: "Order the Military Commissioner's Office to wait on their purchase and have them turned over at Yong Prefecture. We will send troops to care for and feed the elephants as well as have officials take charge of leading them back (?) and protecting them together [with the Annam envoys] all the way to the Camel Paddock where they will be turned over. Nothing is to be disturbed along the route. For the rest operate in accordance with what you estimate. This was the order of the ninth day of the fifth lunar month." (Xu Song 2008: *fanyi*.7.52)

According to another record of this trip, it was allowed because of the goodwill that Lý Thiên Tộ expressed in a memorial of request:

In Qiandao 9.6 (July 10–August 12, 1173), Lý Thiên Tộ sent the envoys Doãn Tử Tứ and Lý Bang Chá to offer local items as tribute. *A howdah for the emperor when riding the elephant, 2,000* jin *of aloeswood incense, eighteen head of thoroughly domesticated elephant cows, an embroidered seating mat for the emperor's use. When the emperor had ascended the throne (July 24, 1162), Thiên Tộ had immediately sent envoys to offer tribute. The border officials made this known to [the court], which then instructed the envoys to go back.*

But on this occasion, he had been so earnest and well prepared, and when he sent this notice of his good intentions, it was allowed. When they arrived, they were housed at the Government Hostel for Soothing Those from Afar. Because the Annam envoys had not come to the capital for a very long time, the Ministry of Rites asked the Bureau of Visitors to inquire about their local customs, their important personages, and the designs on their clothing, in strict conformity with older precedent. (Xu Song 2008: *fanyi*.4.47)

In his geo-ethnography, Zhou Qufei goes into some detail about this trip:

In Qiandao 9 (1173–4) an imperial order commanded Guangxi provincial officials to go to Annam and purchase tame elephants. Because Lý Thiên Tộ had requested to send elephants as tribute, he assented to it, and they sent in five elephants for use in the Great Ritual.[41] The Head Envoy was Esquire for Discussion from Annam, Lý Bang Chánh 李邦正, the Vice Envoy was Esquire of Loyal Assistance of Annam, Nguyễn Văn Hiến 阮元獻.

There were also ten elephants sent to celebrate [Xiaozong's] Ascension to the Gemlike Throne. Grandee of the Inner Guard of Annam, Doãn Tử Tứ (尹子思), was the Head Envoy, and they entered at Yongping Stockade near Zuojiang in Yong Prefecture. Wherever the elephant convoy passed, those prefectures and counties had to bear the costs for holding feasts and providing gifts, for servants, and for elephant houses. And the local militia forces were isolated and lacking any real force and did not have the wherewithal to provoke any awe in foreigners. It was only when the convoy reached Jingjiang – where they met a welcoming contingent dressed in armor and helmets and saw the discipline with which they formed and dispersed their ranks – that the envoys could only utter in praise, "Only after reaching here do we see the impressive dignity of the grand court of the Song." Then, visiting the headquarters, they dismounted and mounted their horses outside of the halberd-gate, and were very respectful in their visit. Fan Chengda was the Marshal at that time,[19] and he adopted a dignified and imposing manner with them. And he was lavish in his banquets and gift-giving.

This section is quite at odds with Fan Chengda's own correspondence to the throne about this visit. He was extremely upset that the envoys did not understand the proper rituals to employ in ordinary exchange with their Song counterparts, and with their lack of refinement. His concerns show not only the lack of discipline in the Jiaozhi delegation, but also a certain relaxation of the expectations that had occurred on the Song side, as well. In a long opinion, he wrote:

> On 11.13 (December 19, 1173), the Military Commissioner of the Western Route in Guangnan [Fan Chengda] made a recommendation,
> In the twenty-sixth year of Shaoxing reign, when Annam sent in tribute, officials from the Commissioner's office went to the lodging of the envoys on a return visit, and as always, transferred cooks, tea, and wine there. I think that all of the Man people under the aegis of the Commissioner from Annam are querulous and need comforting and settling words. When their lesser officials sent on the trip pass by our offices, they are at a loss for a commensurate ritual in response to ours, and I fear that they are as yet not right.
> Therefore, I have carefully consulted the orders from the fifth year of the Xuanhe reign (1123–4), "When tribute missions from Jiaozhi pass through prefectures and military commands they offer no more return rituals." This was never violated later, but the tribute mission of Shaoxing 26 failed to apply this. This time, I am observing the old precedent, and I have ordered Doãn Tử Tứ and others to come to the Commission Office to pay their respects, and after the usual pleasantries of greeting were exchanged, we stopped. And we exchanged calling cards right in the room. There were no more return visits, and the next day we also did not loan them a cook. (Xu Song 2008: *fanyi*.7.54)

Fan then continued with two more recommendations to the court:

> The Military Commissioner of the Western Route in Guangnan, and Magistrate of Jingjiang Precinct, Fan Chengda, made a recommendation,
>> The documents from the Head and Vice-Head of the Convoy, Doãn Tử Tứ and others, have made a request to begin their journey. For all the northern Prefectures and Military Districts that they might pass, I request that all expenses for greetings, great feasts, partings, and associated costs (?) be proportionately calculated and set. This

---

[19] Fan Chengda had been appointed as Military Commissioner of Guangxi in Qiandao 7.4 (May 7–June 5, 1171) and immediately returned home to Wu (Yu Beishan 2006: 147, 148 n. 2, 149 n. 3). According to Fan's diary, he left Wu on December 23, 1172 and arrived to assume his position on April 16, 1173 (Fan Chengda 2002: 60).

can decrease expenditures for detaining people, for harassing incidents, and for incidentals. I have also prepared a document according to which all Routes, Prefectures, and Military Districts should carry this out.
On the same day Military Commissioner of the Western Route in Guangnan, Fan Chengda, made a recommendation,

> The Head and Vice-Head envoys of Annam, Doãn Tử Tứ and others, are sending tribute of their regional items. They arrived in Jingjiang Prefecture on the twenty-second day, and according to the precedent of the twenty-sixth year of Shaoxing, I loaned them seventy-five soldiers of various ranks [for bearers] and fifty-three soldiers of various ranks for a protection guard; these are to be replaced prefecture by prefecture. (Xu Song 2008: *fanyi*.7.54)

Zhou Qufei's account, which may not have been privy to these administrative requests and replies, simply mentions Fan's lavish treatment of the delegation and then goes on.

> On this trip, in addition to presenting elephants, they also sent as tribute gold and silver washbasins, rhinoceros' horns, elephant teeth, superior and inferior aloeswood incense, and the like. The total worth of goods was calculated at only 20 or 30,000 bolts of silk – it did not seem to match the abundance of the Shaoxing tribute. Yet their state had to scour their treasuries and storehouses before they could get it all together. The [Song] court was superabundant in what they returned as gifts, but [the envoys] became greedy for more special treatment. Wherever the Head Envoys and the 100 underlings passed through, the prefectures and districts had to supply and pay them in accordance with government contracts they were issued. They obtained rice to fill up their grain quota, but if they got cash, they would provide each person ten cash per day, and then hoard the rest to take back to their country. The prefectures and districts along the entire road were responsible for providing 800 miscellaneous servants. Only a few actually carried the tribute goods, and the rest were solely for carrying the goods that envoys to wanted to sell on the way to the capital.
>   Elephants can actually float, but at every water crossing the mahouts would find boats to ferry the elephants; only after mahouts were given money would they drive the elephants to swim across. The more polite and ritually correct the accompanying [Song] convoy aides were, the more arrogant became the envoys. Later they had to dispense with any politeness before the envoys would heed their orders. Once these envoys had finagled status as a supplicant feudal state, then they begged for an official seal. Later on, envoys sent to express their appreciation [for the munificence of the Song] kept coming to Qin Prefecture, and they requested several times to send tribute, but none of them were granted. (Zhou Qufei 1999: 58–9)

These last few paragraphs point out how the envoys from Annam were characterized as lacking refinement, arrogant, and greedy. There was, in fact, normally a several-day training and rehearsal period when the delegations arrived in the capital from the south before any kind of meeting was carried out. All ritual and polite behavior needed for inter-action with Offices in Charge of Convoys, the imperial visit, receipt of gifts in their hostels, imperially sponsored feasts, and presentation of convoy goods were comprehensively rehearsed. Provisions were also made for envoys to exchange private goods that they had brought and to purchase items in Lin'an. This was done after a careful calculation of current market value and always with an intermediary from the Director of either the government hostel or the Office of Visitors. Neither were the envoys free to visit Buddhist monasteries or even to sightsee without obtaining a directive and an accompanying responsible official (Xu Song 2008: *zhiguan*.35.13–15).

The Song had a continuing need for these imported elephants for major sacrifices in the year, and the Gaozong emperor had been particularly keen on carrying on the practices of earlier emperors. He remarked constantly in his conversations, decrees, and rescripts about the necessity of following those practices of "the times of our ancestors" (*zuzong shi* 祖宗時), so it would make sense that he would make full use of earlier imperial symbols of power like the elephant to impress on the minds of his people that the reestablished dynasty in Hangzhou was the legitimate perpetuator of traditions. Although both Gaozong and Xiaozong were keen at first on importing elephants, Hangzhou soon proved an impossible place to house them. In Bianliang (modern Kaifeng), the Garden of the Jade Ford had been a huge complex spread out across the level and dry northern plain. Elephants and other rare animals were free to roam there, and they could be enjoyed by officials and visitors – it was actually a kind of zoo but was closed, except on special occasions, to all but imperial and official functions.[20]

Hangzhou, as we have seen, had not been a consensual choice for a capital. It was set between the West Lake on its western side, the Qiantang River on the east, mountains to the south, and marshland to the north. Maps contemporary with the Southern Song do not clearly show the environs of the city. But an artist's rendering of Hangzhou, dated to the 1930s, clearly shows from a bird's-eye perspective the problems inherent in the topography of Lin'an and its environs (Wu Bin and Hangzhou shi Dang'an guan 2006: 121). Large

---

[20] In Xiangfu 5.4 (April–May 1012), it was decreed, "All lions, tame elephants, and other rare beasts sent in tribute from various states should be arranged in gardens outside [of the city walls]. Instruct the many officials to go to these gardens to feast and roam" (Xu Song 2008: *fangyu*.3.17).

open areas for grazing simply did not exist. Elephants were housed in several different locations, including pastureland shared with horses between the southern wall of Hangzhou and the mountains that rise just south of there. A small strip of riverine land was available along the Qiantang River and in the foothills of the mountains on the west.

Compared to sources on elephants for the capital in the north, those from Hangzhou tend to be both few and repetitive. We know of the following locations in Hangzhou where the Elephant Compound was housed (Figure 6):

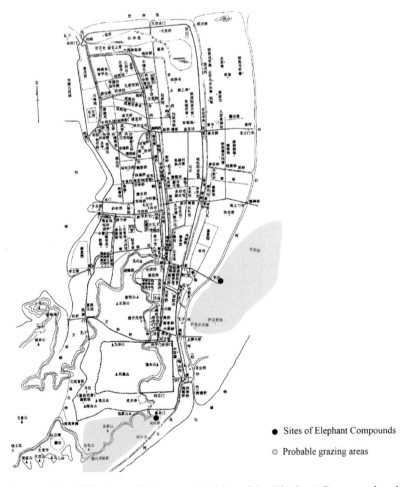

● Sites of Elephant Compounds

○ Probable grazing areas

Figure 6 Probable sites of offices and stables of the Elephant Compound and grazing areas. Sohu.com. Open access.

1. "Elephant Compound: Outside of Jiahui Gate, in the Compound of Imperial Steeds. *In the Jiading era (1208–25) three elephants sent in tribute from Annam were cared for there.*" (Qian Shuiyou 2006: 9.6a)
2. "The Protecting the Sage Army: East of the former elephant compound outside of Chongxin Gate." (Qian Shuiyou 2006: 14.4b)
3. "Baoxiang Monastery: In the seventh year of the Tianfu reign [of the Later Jin, 943] Shi Guangqing gave up his estate to create a monastery, which was named Chongfu Monastery in the past. Later it was changed to its current designation. In the fifteenth year of Shaoxing (1145–46), its land was given over to the Elephant Compound of the Camel Ward, and it was moved to its current location." (Qian Shuiyou 2006, 81.2a)[21]
4. "Pujue Monastery: Constructed in the third year of Qiande by the Qian family. Formerly named Ende, its name was changed to its current title in the middle of the Dazhong xiangfu years. In the fifteenth year of Shaoxing, by imperial order the vacant land in its park was allocated to the Elephant Compound of the Camel Ward." (Qian Shuiyou 2006, 81.7a)

An account from a text on Hangzhou written between 1225 and 1260 also locates the Elephant Compound outside of Chongxin Gate:

> A foreign country has brought six elephants and two camels. Among these is a cow that is called "Third Little Girl," and an Elephant Compound was constructed outside of the gate of Jian bridge (i.e., Chongxin Gate). Each day the elephants followed the officials who were paying court to the front of the palace gates to trumpet a greeting; they returned only after the morning audience was finished. In front of these elephants were several squadrons of drummers and gong-beaters, along with thirty or forty flags of different colors. A person rode on the back of each elephant, wearing a small cap and holding a pick, dressed in a purple robe. All the people in the retinue wore robes and caps, struck the drums, and rang the gongs in the middle of the road to lead them back to the elephant compound. (Xihu laoren 1956: 121)

We can actually trace this activity on a map found in a 1268 gazetteer of Hangzhou (Figure 7).

As in Bianliang, elephants in Hangzhou continued to be used in grand imperial rituals. Eyewitness accounts from Hangzhou are very specific about the rituals, and about the use of elephants. For instance, in his description of Hangzhou, Zhou Mi 周密 (1232–98), wrote:

---

[21] Wu Zhijing 1980: 1.12 has the following information: "The Vinaya Chongfu Monastery of the Sacred Fungus is in the Chongxin Gate Alley in the Eastern Flower Garden. It is commonly designated as the Candle Cloister. In the year *jiyou* of the Zhenguan reign in the Tang (649–50) Shi Guangqing gave up his estate to build the Shiji Monastery. The Song dynasty Chan Monk, Foyin (1032–98), rebuilt it."

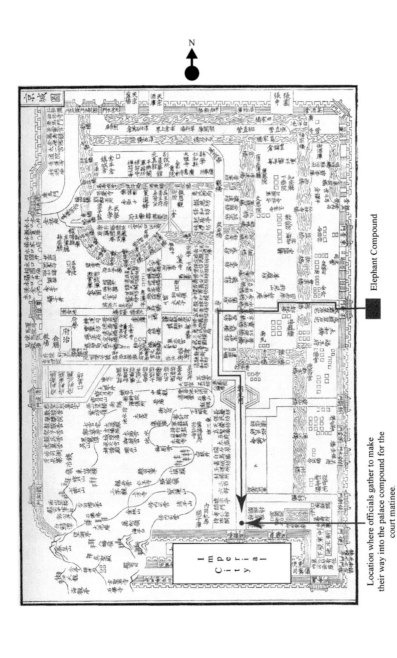

N

Elephant Compound

Location where officials gather to make
their way into the palace compound for the
court matinee.

Figure 7 Probable route of elephants who accompany morning audience at court. Author's adapted version of a map from 1268 gazetteer of Hangzhou. Title: *Gazetteer of Lin'an during the Xianchun Reign of the Southern Song* (Xianchun Lin'an zhi; 咸淳臨安志). www.loc.gov/item/2021666450/. Library of Congress, World Digital Library. Open access.

Great Ritual Ceremonies: Suburban Sacrifice; the Bright Hall

There is one Suburban Sacrifice every three years. Prior to that year, an edict is promulgated on New Year's Day to hold the sacrifice on the winter solstice in the southern suburbs; or they could carry out the sacrifice on the next New Year's Day. *For the Bright Hall the edict is promulgated only six months earlier, and the ceremony is held on the first* xin *day of the last month of autumn.* In the fifth or sixth month of the year a day is picked *on which to order the leader* of the Fiscal Commission and the Palace Maintenance Office to refurbish and decorate the suburban altar and to wrap and knot [the curtain walls] for the Green City Fasting Palace and other buildings – in all several hundred bays in size. These were all covered with rush mats and protected with green cloth.

Civil officials and soldiers were simultaneously dispatched to repair and pack any muddy roads from, first, the Ancestral Temple to the Gate of Offering Sacrifice [at the entrance to the Altar to Heaven] and then, from Jiahui Gate to Lizheng Gate, all totaling some 9 *li* and 320 *bu* (±5.15 km or 3.52 miles). *For the Bright Hall, it was only from the Ancestral Temples to the Lizheng Gate.* The roads were all filled and packed with sand left from the tidal bore. They were as flat as a feast mat, all to make the five carts' travel back and forth convenient.

Each unit had a "lead singer," who was marked by a colored flag, and who sang in harmony the "Pestle Song" and others in order to match all of the cadences [of those pulling carts].[22] Residents along both sides of the two roads would fête them with colored strips of cloth, cash, and wine. Moreover, the Elephant Court was ordered to train the elephants, leading them with a vermilion flag, keeping time with two metal gongs and three drums. Each elephant had a rider, dressed in purple robes and a hat with long tails, carrying a short billhook in their hands. The elephants circled around, knelt, and rose completely in accord with the mind of their human rider. The marketplaces took advantage of this to hustle to sell little elephant papercuts or clay models for people to purchase and give [to relatives and friends].

There were five carts, each loaded with iron – as heavy as 10,000 *jin* (±6,000 kilograms) – but proportional to the weight of the cart, to test the forces of speed and wobble. This was done a month before being presented, and it was denoted as "the test of stability." On the day before the entourage left, a large colored room was tied together in front of the Grand Ancestral Palace, and the carts were placed there to allow the citizens of the capital to look at them.

From the month prior, one by one, in order, the entourage was rehearsed daily without fail. Ten days before the suburban sacrifice, all of the officials in charge as well as those officials who were ancillary to the feast were all warned of punishments for failure in their duties by the Chancellery. *Members of the royal family were counseled in the Great Ancestral Hall.*

---

[22] This was a song by workers who used heavy pestles to pound the loess soil to the typical *terre pisé* walls; they were able to thus keep a cadence to work in synchronicity.

Three days prior, the Hundred Officials formally request the August Emperor to go to fast in the Daqing Hall. On this day, the emperor wears a "hat that reaches to the heavens,"[23] ties up his jade pendants,[24] and ascends the high throne. Inner servants formally request he come down from his seat and go to the fasting rooms. On the next day, the imperial carriage visits the Jingling Palace,[25] and the emperor wears his formal robes and headgear to perform the ritual. *The retinue is the same as that on the Four Seasonal Prime Sacrifices.* At the conclusion of the ritual, the emperor returns and goes straightaway to the fasting hall to fast overnight. On this eve, at the fourth drum (1–3 a.m.) the emperor dons his formal robe and hat and visits each of the rooms of the various ancestors to perform the rituals of the court feast. (Zhou Mi 2007: 12–14)

A similar account occurs in a 1274 work entitled *A Record of a Dream That Passes in the Time That Millet Cooks*, which describes the ceremonies in a quite different way.

Rehearsing Carts and Elephants in Years of Solemn Sacrifices

Major sacrifices in the Bright Hall are carried out once every three years. At the beginning of spring a decree is issued to the empire to carry out sacrifices with purity and reverence. On the first *si* day of the ninth month there is a great festal sacrifice to Heaven and Earth in order to pray thanks to the ancestors and to gratefully order the hundred officials to each carry out the duties of their position. This follows the system used by the Sui and Tang dynasties.

At the beginning of summer, muddy roads are repaired and packed down:
Select and dispatch Soldiers of the Feathered Forest in the Three Imperial Guards
To pack down the Imperial Road until it is as smooth as a whetstone.
On the day the Spring ecliptic is perfectly in place, it will illuminate sun and moon,
When the model entourage is strictly prepared it will be able to proceed securely.

Elephants and carts are rehearsed two months prior. The cart goes back and forth every day, and it is tested time and again in front of the Ancestral Hall. It goes to Lizheng Gate and then is returned once to the Court of Carts and Conveyances. If it is simply to test the cart, then each cart is weighed down with a thousand *jin* (about 600 kilograms).

---

[23] A hat that is made of a headband and fifteen standing wires, slanted slightly toward the back and curled on the ends, then covered with a cloth with seams. It is also called a "high mountain hat" and, because of the view of the curled cloth from the side, a "cloud cap." It was worn by the emperor.

[24] So that they do not clink; made silent for the occasion.

[25] Where the portraits and paraphernalia of the prior emperors were kept.

If it is a year for the Southern Suburban Sacrifice, then all five carts are used in rehearsal. Truly, as it is said,

> Ritual carts for imperial use have wheels of five colors,
> Colored hawsers lifted in pairs, familiarly lift up the clouds.
> Far away, the emperor's power is known, awesomely weighty,
> So fine iron must be used, a pressing weight of 10,000 *jin*.

If it is a solemn sacrifice year, then a single cart is used to stand in place of the Jade Cart. Two blue flags are set on the cart along with one drum, it is driven by several horses, and the imperial guards on the two sides of the cart are all in purple robes and small caps. Several people in front of the cart crack whips to move the cart. Several tens of vermilion flags are arranged in front, as well as tens and tens of brass gongs and small and large drums; all the flag bearers and drummers are clothed in purple robes and small caps. Later two elephants were used, each ridden by a single person who wore a cap with long tails that were folded across each other. They wore purple robes, driving the elephant by sitting on its neck, holding a short-handled silver mattock but with a tapered blade (billhook), and the elephant is given a spike if it is not minding well. When they reach the Ancestral Hall and Lizheng Gate, this billhook is used to make the elephants turn in a circle, and after several times of walking like this, they form an even line. They are ordered to bow and ordered to take on the posture of trumpeting a greeting.

Onlookers along the Imperial Avenue are like walls. Those small elephants molded of powdered clay and wood and decorated with a colored ribbon sold through wagering, as well as paper cutouts, are purchased by people from outside areas and given away to others as a local specialty. (Wu Zimu 2001: 49–50)

Elephants lived the majority of their adult lives in service to ritual and spectacle in the capital at Lin'an. They were sometimes paraded to government hostels to be shown off to diplomatic envoys from both the south and north. The following rescript makes clear that this was an expected event of envoys to the capital.

In Shaoxing 14.12.24 (January 4, 1114) the Office in Charge of the Comings and Goings of State Envoys made a recommendation,

According to older precedent, when Northern Envoys [from the Liao and Jin dynasties] arrived in the capital and after they had finished archery rituals in the Garden of the Jade Ford, they would go to observe the tame elephants. Last year, the envoys for the New Year's Celebration never had a chance to look at the elephants. According to a declaration by the Camel Paddock, they ended up leading the elephants to the hostel for viewing. We have carefully considered what happened when the envoys who came for this New Year's Celebration wanted to see the elephants, but the [Camel Paddock] was not prepared as the time approached. We desire that the Camel Paddock always follow precedent in preparing to parade the elephants.

4 Ivory in China and a Stave

During the Middle Ages, the Chinese used hundreds of live Asian elephants in imperial processions. They also used the ivory from a far greater number of elephants, ivory which, like the elephants, arrived in the form of a steady tribute of elephant tusks to the Song state. Under the Song Dynasty, only the state monopoly could sell ivory. A rescript of 977 had already prohibited the private collection or storage of fragrances and medicines, rhinoceros horns and elephant tusks, and these four items were put under a category called "controlled items (榷署)," which were subject to sale only by the state monopoly. But, for several years, depending on the available supply of tusks, they vacillated between being controlled or uncontrolled (非榷署) commodities. In fact, by the early twelfth century the court treasuries were so well stocked with ivory that they used their supply to barter in turn with foreign traders for other luxury goods. In order to maintain the price of domestic ivory, the Song also sold its oversupply to both the foreign Liao and Jin dynasties on the northern frontier and the northern steppe peoples, the Jurchen and Khitan, along with other luxury goods (Zhang Ji 2010: 188 and throughout).

The government, which regulated the ivory trade network, gave penalties for private trading. This was certainly spurred and maintained by the desire for luxury goods among the Song elite (Zhang Ji 2010: 189). Again, trade networks were closely controlled by the government, and the penalties for private trading were severe. As one rescript remarks:

> In the fourth lunar month of the second civil year of the Chunhua reign (May 17–June 14, 991) it was ordered, "There are herds of elephants in the mountain forests of the prefectures of Lei, Hua, Xin, Bai, Hui, and En [Guangdong and Guangxi]. People of the realm can take their tusks, but officials must prohibit them from selling the tusks. From this point forward, people of the realm are ordered to send them to officials, who shall requite them at half of the market price. Those who dare hide them away or secretly sell them to others shall be sentenced according to law." (Xu Song 2008: *shihuo* 37.2.*shiyi*.Taizong. See also Xu Song 2008: *xingfa* 2.*jinyue*.Taizong)

Since this proscription coincides with the development of the Office in Charge of Trade Argosies (市舶司), which was tasked with regulating and taxing imports, we can assume that once the capital was fully supplied with ivory and other luxury items, a stricter control over domestic production would severely restrict Indigenous hunting and supply.

The state not only regulated domestic elephant ivory sources but also restricted private trade from foreign sources. Private trade was confined to officials, prominent families, and foreign traders. This is exemplified by a Persian trader who had brought 299 tusks and 35 rhinoceros horns to the Southern Song court in the 1130s. When he landed in Guangdong, he was approached by a certain Song military officer, named variously in the records as Cao Na 曹納, Cao Ne 曹訥, or Zeng Na 曾納, who offered his daughter up for economic gain. The trader, Puyali 蒲亞里, became quite comfortable about settling in Guangdong, but the emperor employed him as a negotiator to travel back and forth from Tajik to China and to bring in tribute to the court.

In the early years of the Song, much ivory was sourced domestically. There were herds of wild elephants along the riverine areas of China. These caused an enormous problem for agricultural initiatives in the south, and they were in the process of being hunted to extinction (Elvin 2004: 1–19). As populations dwindled due to burgeoning human populations and agricultural pressure, live elephants and ivory were no longer sourced from the herds along the riverine areas. During the Song Dynasty period, ivory arrived from new sources in the southern provinces of modern China, including the yet-to-be-conquered peripheral states in the Jiang-Zhe and Sichuan areas, and, as with live elephants, from Vietnam, including the states of Đinh, Đại Việt, and Champa. Ivory also arrived from other parts of Southeast Asia, including Cambodia, Brunei, Borneo, and Tāmbraliṅga (in the southern arm of modern Thailand). Ivory trade networks also included the southeastern portion of India and the Persian-speaking kingdoms of Khurasan, Transoxiana, and Tajik (early Oxus valley cultures) (see Zhang Ji 2010: 188 and throughout).

In the tenth century, although it had it previously sourced ivory from its own elephants, China sought supplies from abroad. The early Song attempted to increase foreign trade and, from the *Edited Administrative Documents from the Song*, we find an interesting note from the summer of 987:

> In the fifth lunar month of the fourth civil year of the Yongxi reign (May 30–June 28, 987), [those in charge] dispatched eight men who were Inner Servants [eunuchs who served in the emperor's private bureaucracy] who had been given imperial directives. Gold and clothing were divided [among those each in charge of one] of four convoy networks. Each went to one of the many foreign states in the southern oceans to solicit import goods, and to purchase scents and fragrances, rhinoceros horns and elephant tusks, real pearls, and borneol camphor. Each convoy was provided an imperial rescript, left empty of addressees, which could be filled out and granted at any place they reached. (Xu Song 2008: *zhiguan* 44.*Shibo si.zhiguan* 44.2ª)

Tribute missions involved heavy gifting in response from the Song court and were a form of foreign trade. Trade missions, when they reached one of the southern ports – Canton, Guilin in Guangxi, Hangzhou, or Mingzhou – met with officials from an office known as the Office in Charge of Trade Argosies, who taxed the vessel an entry tax of 10 percent of the cargo's estimated value. Since these were often luxury items, the government monopolized their sale in the Song lands, and these were further taxed as the government sold them to influential or noble families. A price was set on a percentage of the value of goods imported and then either purchased or bartered on that value by government officials, who further monopolized the sale of such goods.[26]

Muslim merchants, who were notoriously wealthy in Guangzhou (Lu Yun 2014: 55, 50), sourced ivory from Africa. Although the Portuguese and Chinese had not yet established the sea routes of the fifteenth century, by the twelfth century, China increasingly shifted from ivory supplied from Southeast Asia and India to ivory sourced from African elephants. Ivory from Asian elephants was considered substandard. Twelfth-century Chinese sources describe Asian ivory as too small and having an unfortunate brown tint. Chóu K'ü-feï [Zhou Qufei], as assistant subprefect in Kui-lin [Guilin], wrote in 1178 that in contrast to the small, low-quality tusks from Tonking, the northern region of Vietnam, and Cambodia, the African variety was "great ivory" (qtd. in Laufer 1925: 15).

The Song considered African elephant ivory to be of superior quality. Puyali, the twelfth-century Persian trader who traveled back and forth from Tajik in Central Asia, most likely sourced ivory from African ivory networks to meet Song demand. As early as the tenth century, the historian Al-Mas'ūdī (ca. 893–956), based in Baghdad, complained that foreign markets like the Song paid such a high price for Zanzibar-sourced elephant ivory from Arab merchants that no supplies were reaching his homeland (Laufer 1925: 15). The historian also points to ivory overconsumption in China by stating that no person in China would present himself in the palace to the king unless they were carried in on an ivory palanquin.

The growth of an ivory art industry in China began after the later Mongol period, was spurred in part perhaps by the Yuan love of ivory goods. In the Southern Song region, however, ivory artifacts were largely utilitarian. In demand for the Ivory Office 象牙局, elephant tusks were made into everyday objects, including toys, chess pieces, hairpins, and *huban*, the ivory staves of office (Cai Tao 1983: 70). To conclude our discussion of elephants and ivory in China, we examine one of these staves and propose a biogeography for the elephant that provided the ivory. We argue that the stave is from Asian elephant ivory, which was described by Chóu K'ü-feï as a "lower"-quality grade.

In Ma Hezhi's 馬和之 (1130–70) painting to accompany the *Canon of Filial Piety*, written in the hand of the Southern Song emperor known as Gaozong, we see several officials dressed in court garb, each holding an ivory stave (Figure 8). In contrast to ecclesiastical ivories produced in Christian Europe,

---

[26] Apparently, among the imports, the only thing allowed to be sold directly to nongovernmental persons was medicinal herbs.

Figure 8 Quadrant of Ma Hezhi's (1130–70) plates for the *Canon of Filial Piety*.
National Palace Museum, Taipei.
Open access.

this was essentially a piece of office equipment used in audiences between the emperor and his court officials. The side facing the official was used for notes, either those prepared as prompts for presenting a proposition to the emperor, or for noting down his responses.

But some further information is needed to understand what this stave means in a larger context. Traditional Confucianism mandates a hierarchical set of ethical correlations based on "Five Constants," a set of metonymical correlations – ruler–minister; father–son; husband–wife; elder brother–younger brother; friend–friend – that suggest an ideal combination of reciprocal relationships in which compassion is bestowed by the superior while filial and obedient behavior is reciprocated from the inferior. These constants extended as well into ritual, institutional, and governmental behavior, all of which were thought to be an extension outward of a human subject always in the state of perfecting itself ethically. Inward development produced a moral power others sought to imitate. This attraction resulted in a presumed sequence: the ethical development of an individual resulted in an ordered family that became part of a state in harmony, all together producing a world at peace. This spectrum was sequential only in the following sense: the growth of each sphere of develop-ment always contained within it the ethical "becoming" of all other spheres and at the center always remained a self in the process of moral growth, acting according to the ethical demands of their position within the hierarchy of relationships.

The stave (called *hu* or *huban* 笏板 in Chinese) symbolized the relationship between ruler and minister and by the twelfth and thirteenth centuries had been in use for more than two millennia. As one might expect in such a hierarchically ordered world, sumptuary rules governed the eighteen clas-sifications (1a through 9b) of an exquisitely structured civil bureaucracy, each stratum of which was assigned specific kinds and colors of implements, robes, and conveyances – even to the kind of jade pendants and pouches suspended from the belt of their court robes. And each official held the appropriate stave. All of this was stipulated by ritual codes. While sumptuary rules may have changed slightly over time, by the thirteenth century, specific materials were designated for the staves of office, held by all civil bureaucrats.

Any official above the rank of 5b used an ivory stave (Toqto et al. 1985: vol. 11, 3569). These staves were carried on virtually every public occasion (Figure 9). Since the Song bureaucracy counted a steady annual number of 20,000 ranked civil servants, the production of such staves must have been difficult to supply. There are few ivory staves remaining from the Song dynasty period, and those that survive have suffered the ravages of time.

It is only at the end of the fourteenth century that the carving of these implements is considered anything except utilitarian. With the increasing importation of African ivory that followed the famous Zheng He expeditions of the fifteenth century, ivory carving seems to have been elevated from craftsmanship to art. Verifiable staves from the Song are exceptionally rare and often mistaken in auction catalogs for staves from the fourteenth century, but we are safe in assuming on the basis of textual evidence that *huban* from the late fourteenth century were similar in shape and size. A superb example is found in the Palace Museum in Taipei (Figure 10).

Figure 9 Parade to perform the Suburban Sacrifices to Heaven. Date: perhaps eleventh century. Medium: Part of a scroll entitled "The Grand Imperial Retinue: Picture and Text (大鹵簿圖書)." This portion displays the civil and military offices as well as eunuch members of the emperor's personal staff. Each of the riders on the left side carries a stave. National Museum of China. Open access.

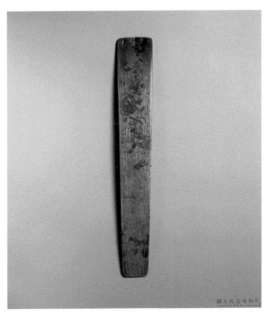

Figure 10 Ming Dynasty ivory *hu* stave. Dimensions: length 45 cm; width 5.7 cm. Assigned date 1368–1644. Medium: elephant ivory. Maker: unclear. National Palace Museum, Taipei. Open access.

Despite existing examples, the biogeography in this case is not based on an existing artifact in a museum. Rather, we name and offer a possible life story of Y Khun, the Asian elephant that provided the ivory for one of the unidentified staves produced during the Southern Song dynasty. We chose the Vietnamese name "Y Khun" for this elephant, a name that recognizes the hill tribes and languages that provide names to captured elephants. In 2015, a fifty-four-year-old bull named Y Khun was being raised in a sanctuary in Vietnam ("Owner" 2015). In early China, the Vietnamese name of the elephant would remain for the elephant's life because their mahouts accompanied tribute missions and remained in China for at least as long as the elephant was alive. While the exact circumstances of the elephant's life are unknown, we construct his life based on the late twelfth-century Song order for ten male elephants with young teeth and fine tusks to serve in the imperial state ceremony in the capital (see p. 31). Behind the unidentified stave was a living, breathing elephant, a robust consciousness of life itself that we shall create in what follows in the form of Y Khun, a bull sent from Đại Việt in Annam to the Song court in 1173.

Aside from exportation, some ivory tusks came in attached to living bodies that had traversed the landmass of southeastern and northern Asia, sent as tribute beasts from the same countries supplying tusks and rhinoceros horns.

Y Khun was one of the many tame Asian elephants sent to the Song court as tribute from these countries as a symbol of their status as protectorates of the Song state or as supplicant trading partners. There are enough written accounts extant for us to provide a plausible scenario for tracking Y Khun from his capture in the highlands of northern Vietnam, through his use in the imperial rituals, to his release as he grew aged, and finally his demise – from a vital young body to death and dismemberment, and then to simple artifact.

The description of the complex system of tribute from the administrative documents of the Song Dynasty offers the scenario in which Y Khun was brought from Vietnam in 1173, as recounted in Section 3. He was taken away from his homeland by a request to send elephants to the southern capital of Hangzhou in 1172, in response to which the Military Commission of the Western Route of Guangnan gathered ten male elephants with young teeth and fine tusks for the Great Ritual. Y Khun was probably captured somewhere in the forests south-southeast of modern Hanoi. After Y Khun endured training, he was chosen to be sent as tribute to the Song state, where he would be further trained to take part in ritual parades and sacrifices such as the triennial sacrifice to Heaven, held at the Altar of Heaven.

Y Khun's life was set in the later middle period of the Song Dynasty and subject to the ideological calculus of elephant, emperor, and power. He lived the majority of his adult life in service to ritual and spectacle in the capital. He was sometimes paraded to government hostels to be shown off to diplomatic envoys from both the south and north. His sense of time was dictated by Song ritual and institutional time; he was hemmed in by the small spaces of Hangzhou, taken out only for parades and for spectacle.

Before his tooth was used to carve a stave, Y Khun may have grown old. Perhaps as his other teeth grew too long, having been deprived of the natural wear that stripping branches and trunks would have provided, he was sent to live out his days in a Buddhist monastery. Perhaps Y Khun died in the thirteenth century after spending the end of his life there, surrounded by compassionate care. Rather than being poked by his handlers to ensure compliance, he may have been cleaned regularly, a process which held another human significance, in which one tries to scrub the elephant and scrub away the myriad forms of mental and material constructs (also called *xiang* 象) that occupy the mind. The same phrase for washing the elephant (洗象) also meant "to cleanse phenomena from the mind," and it became a favorite motif of painters (Figure 11). Symbols or signs in the Buddhist sense of the mental images that humans create as materiality in the mind – no matter how ethereally – stand in the way of complete emptiness.

Figure 11 *Washing the Elephant*, attributed to Qian Xuan (1232–99). Smithsonian Institute. Open access CC0.

Upon his death, Y Khun's hide and tusks were removed, the hide to be worked into flexible strips or become a tough covering for the shields of war. His tusks were sent to the Ivory Office and made into a stave. His remains went back into the human world, made into combs and chess pieces, as well as a functional tool of office, becoming symbolic once more as it denoted its bearer's status. The stave was perhaps gifted to a royal prince by the family of his bride-to-be or given to a high official or foreign envoy as a special imperial gift.

We imagine that what is left of Y Khun's tusk now is a carved artifact, now a thousand years old, circulating in anonymity among collectors or forgotten in a museum. No memory is left of the magnificent beast who had marched 2,500 kilometers from his jungle home near Hanoi to the lively streets of Hangzhou, there to live in service to the ritual needs of humans, forced to march, wheel, trumpet, and kneel on cruel command, caparisoned and paraded for spectacle. Nothing of him remains but a curved wedge of ivory, smooth to the touch.

5 Elephants and Ivory in Iberia

In radical contrast to China, very few elephants walked alive in Europe in the Middle Ages. In 1583, King Philip II of Spain traveled from Lisbon to Madrid with an Indian elephant. In a biogeography, Beusterien (2020b) names him "Hawa'i," connecting Philip II's elephant to his place of origin because Akbar (1542–1605), the ruler of the Mughal empire, called his favorite elephant by that name. Descriptions from the period describe Hawa'i as "tame" and claim he obeyed everything that his mahout ordered. Like the elephant, texts from the period leave the driver anonymous. The mahout is only described as a "noble Black man." Philip II later gifted Hawa'i to the king of France, who then regifted the pachyderm to Queen Elizabeth of England. The elephant spent his last days in the menagerie at the Tower of London and died in 1592 (Beusterien 2020b: 43).[27]

Philip II commissioned a goldsmith, Juan de Arfe (1535–1603), to represent his 1583 arrival in Madrid as a glorious sign of victory. Arfe chose to decorate a ewer (an elaborately crafted metal water pitcher) to represent the elephant. He does not depict the mahout, but, instead, a two-story box on the elephant, a typical image in the period to indicate a war elephant. The elephant engraved on the ewer marches in a Roman victory parade, in which the Spanish king Philip II is portrayed in the guise of Hannibal's most famous adverary, the Roman victor Scipio Africanus (236–183 BCE). Charles I, Philip II's father, was also interested in elephants as a sign of regal power. He had previously paraded an Indian elephant in Valladolid (in 1542), and, like his Habsburg son, had commissioned another rendering of Scipio Africanus. Instead of a gilded silver water pitcher, King Charles commissioned the representation of Scipio as part of a magnificent tapestry cycle to be woven in Brussels (Beusterien 2020b: 96–97n.105).

Keen to portray Scipio Africanus as a mirror for themselves, the Spanish Habsburgs represented the Roman general as prince of an all-powerful empire. In their telling of the legend of Scipio, he was not only a wise military tactician and emblem of imperial triumph but also a tamer of elephants, who were symbols of the power of a prince over the enemy. Scipio, designated as Roman proconsul of Spain, was renowned as the brilliant victor over Carthage's armies in Iberia, and his military success was tied to elephants. First, he conquered them: in the decisive battle that marked Rome's ejection of Carthage from Spain, Scipio ignored the line of elephants at the center of the Carthaginian troops and attacked the flanks, defeating Hannibal's brother. Following Scipio's victory, his military descendants, in turn, brought the now-extinct North African breed of elephants to Iberia as part of military campaigns, just as the Carthaginians had done previously, to lead military campaigns to quell Indigenous Celtiberians. For one Iberian campaign, a Roman general acquired elephants from Masinissa (r. ca. 202–148 BCE), the first Numidian

---

[27] The Tower menagerie's origins can be traced to 1235, when the Holy Roman Emperor Frederick II gifted three leopards to Henry III of England (Harris 2020: 65). Frederick famously kept a menagerie of his own animals which, aside from his elephant and large African cats, included a polar bear, camels, and a giraffe (Heng 2018: 254n.67).

king, and another general acquired elephants from King Jugurtha (r. 118–105 BCE), Masinissa's grandson (Kistler 2006: 157–158). Jugurtha's elephants were used to stop the famed Celtiberian resistance at Numancia, an event that had achieved the status of a national legend during Charles and Philip's reigns over 1,500 years later.

Indigenous elephants in Spain and neighboring northern African species had been extinct for more than a thousand years when Charles I came to power in Spain at the beginning of the sixteenth century.[28] All the elephants that arrived in the Iberian Peninsula (and Europe) in the sixteenth century, some twenty in number, were Asian. They were supplied via Portuguese vessels. Each arrived with at least one mahout. For instance, one driver, Gaspar, traveled from Goa; King John III of Portugal granted him freedom in 1559 – evidence that he led a life of captivity like his elephant companion (Jordan Gschwend and Lowe 2017: 332).[29]

In thirteenth-century China, the Mongols, a people from the Central Asian steppes, controlled the world's largest contiguous land empire. They completed a series of military victories that culminated in the Yuan Dynasty, which began in 1271. The vast expanse of land that they controlled facilitated the commerce of Asian and African ivory along the Silk Road back to China. The Mongols also exported live elephants, not for war, but for processions.

In contrast to Mongol and Song China, which used hundreds of live elephants in ceremonies during the period, only three live elephants were brought to Europe between 801 and 1450. Each arrived because of diplomacy with Egypt. In ninth-century Egypt, elephants had been extinct for about 500 years. The North African species had also been exterminated in the Roman period, and, while ivory arrived from the sub-Sahara, tamed elephants did not. Ottoman caliphs in Byzantium and Egypt, who cherished live animal menageries, obtained live Asian elephants. Moreover, those Asian elephants were in precious short supply. Ottoman courtiers who wanted a prestige elephant to give as tribute had to rely on Indian potentates, who kept access to the prized living gifts scarce (Ottewill-Soulsby 2023: 129).

---

[28] The last indigenous elephants on the Iberian Peninsula went extinct some 10,000 years ago. Around 17,000 years ago, as evidenced by cave paintings at Altamira and El Pindal in the north of Spain, humans lived alongside now-extinct Iberian species of elephants. Excavations reveal that prehistoric people in Spain processed ivory objects from the now-extinct elephant species from northern Africa, including sandals, votive axe heads, and combs in the Copper (ca. 3200–2300 BCE), Bronze (2300–700 BCE), and Iron Age (700–1 BCE) (Mas García 1987; Luciañez Triviño 2018; Barciela González et al. 2022).

[29] Prior to Philip and Charles, Manuel, king of Portugal, collected elephants of state and used them in ceremonial processions in Lisbon. He used also used them in prestige diplomacy, sending one as a gift to the king of Java and another, the white elephant Hanno, to the pope.

Charlemagne (748–814) united Christendom in western Central Europe three centuries after the fall of the Western Roman Empire. The courts of Charlemagne and his successors carved elephant ivory into Christian icons as aspirational objects for church and state leaders that revived Roman formats and styles. They sometimes repurposed tablets that had been carved in the Roman period but primarily acquired new ivory sources via routes from East Africa.

Like other members of medieval global elites, Charlemagne not only sought out high-quality ivory but also desired a live elephant as a sign of imperial power. He successfully acquired a single Indian elephant during his reign. An Egyptian prince acquired an Indian elephant and gave Charlemagne the animal as a gift as part of a diplomatic package (Nees 2006; Ottewill-Soulsby 2023). The diplomatic gift was the result of Charlemagne's diplomacy with Hārūn al-Rashīd (766–809), Baghdad caliph of the ʿAbbāsid dynasty. Charlemagne named his elephant after Abū al-ʿAbbās al-Saffāḥ (722–54), Islamic caliph (r. 749–54) and first of the ʿAbbāsid dynasty: The *Annales regni francorum* (802) notes: "nomen elefanti erat Abul Abaz" (the name of the elephant was Abū al-ʿAbbās) (qtd. in Cobb 2021: 51n.6).

The elephant Abū al-ʿAbbās walked from Baghdad to Alexandria, Egypt, on foot and then arrived by boat at Pisa, from where the animal walked to Pavia to meet Charlemagne. Having traveled with Isaac, his Jewish North African mahout, the Indian elephant is reputed to have swum in the Rhine River near his stables in Augsburg and lived in Charlemagne's court for about eight years. Abū al-ʿAbbās died in Augsburg in 810.

Over three centuries later, in 1229, Al-Malik al-Kāmil (1180–1238), the Ayyūbid sultan who ruled Egypt (as well as Palestine and Syria), gave Frederick II, also Holy Roman Emperor (1194–1250), another prestige gift of a live elephant. At this period of medieval history, European Christian powers focused the attention of the crusades against the "infidel" not on Jerusalem, but Egypt. The Egyptian Saladin (Ṣalāḥ al-Dīn Yūsuf ibn Ayyūb, ca. 1137–93), the founder of the Ayyūbid dynasty, had wrested Jerusalem from Latin Christendom in 1187. Saladin's success turned Europe's geopolitical focus in the thirteenth century to Egypt (Heng 2018: 226). Al-Kāmil's gift of the elephant to the Holy Roman Emperor sought to appease the new crusaders who had set out to conquer Egypt. The German Holy Roman Emperor marched with the elephant back through Europe in a show of regal pride. In Cremona in northern Italy, for instance, Frederick II celebrated the visit of his brother-in-law, the English prince Richard of Cornwall (1209–72), by marching the elephant in a triumphal parade.

The third live elephant to have walked in medieval Europe was contemporaneous with the second. The gift elephant was also supplied from Egypt. The sultan Shajar al-Durr (d. 1250) – and Aybak (Al-Mu'izz 'Izz al-Dīn al-Manṣūr Aybak, r. 1254–7), whom she appointed as commander-in-chief – appear to have arranged the gift package for Louis IX of France (1214–70) as part of a truce and prisoner exchange (Folda 2005: 247). Louis IX had led the last crusade (the Seventh, from 1244–54), and his military campaign in Egypt had failed, and as a result he was held in captivity in Palestine for four years (Jackson 2007). As part of a treaty with the Cairo potentates, Shajar and Aybak sent the gift package, which included the remains of Christian soldiers and captives as well as a live elephant, to King Louis (Folda 2005: 247).[30] Louis traveled by land back to France, whereupon he promptly gifted the elephant in 1255 to King Henry III of England, who had arrived in Paris for an extended stay to visit his brother-in-law (Carpenter 2020: 611). The elephant survived for about three years and, like Philip II's Hawa'i in the sixteenth century, also died in the royal menagerie in the Tower of London.

Rome had brought elephants to fight in Spain in the ancient period. In the late medieval period, Iberia was responsible for shipping the first live elephants to Europe from Asia. Prior to the fifteenth century, no live elephant had set foot in Spain for a millennium. In the thirteenth century, elephant remains arrived in the form of ivory sourced from sub-Saharan Africa. A survey of the use of ivory in the reign of King Alfonso X of Castile (also called the Wise), the monarch who played foundational role in standardizing Spanish on the Iberian Peninsula after centuries of Islamic rule, provides a window onto how medieval Spain reduced elephants to the symbolic value of their tusks, wherein they still served as war animals and signs of power.

Alfonso made Seville the capital of Castile and León in 1248. The kingdoms of Castile and León under Alfonso received most of Iberia's supply of ivory in the thirteenth century. Just as Egypt provided live elephants in the thirteenth century, so it also provided elephant ivory. Alfonso, shortly after the French king Louis IX's failed Latinizing crusade to Egypt, established diplomatic relations with the sultanate. Alfonso had largely consolidated the Christian presence on the Iberian Peninsula after his father King Ferdinand III of Castile (ca. 1199/1201–1252) had conquered Seville. He converted the former Almohad capital into a fortified Christian one, and he looked to an alliance with Egypt as he focused imperial ambitions on North Africa (he sent expeditions out from the newly occupied Cadiz and the Puerto of Santa María to secure port cities in North Africa such as Salé, adjacent to Rabat in Morocco).

---

[30] The Rothelin Continuation, a collection of crusader manuscripts, mentions that an elephant and an *onagre* were included as part of the gift package (Rothelin Continuation II 1859: 625). The *onagre* was probably not a wild ass (as proposed in the translation by Shirley 1999: 110), but a zebra.

In Iberia, the Islamic stronghold in Andalusia was in retreat in the thirteenth century. The Almohad Dynasty had controlled Iberia for over a century (1147–1269), and King Alfonso had a vested interest in ending its power. To this end, an alliance with the newly formed Malmuk Sultanate (1250–1517) served his geopolitical interest in keeping at bay other growing regional dynasties such as the Marinid dynasty, who established control in western Maghrib and took over Fez and Marrakesh in 1248 (Ilahiane 2006: xxi). Egypt, in turn, with the power shift from the emirs of Cordoba to the newly established stronghold of Seville as capital, looked to Iberia to increase its geopolitical sphere of influence.

In an act of diplomacy, an ambassadorial delegation from Cairo arrived at Alfonso's court at Seville in December of 1260, sent by the sultan Qutuz (al-Malik al-Muẓaffar Sayf ad-Dīn Quṭuz, d. 1260), Shajar and Aybak's successor (Ballesteros Berreta 1934: 36–37). A miniature from Alfonso's *Las Cantigas*, a series of songs dedicated to the Virgin Mary of Christian culture, depicts the gift tribute sent by the Egyptian sultan. It includes a giraffe, zebra (the first illustration of its kind in Europe), and a kneeling tusked elephant (Figure 12). Specimens of live animals brought as part of prestige tribute packages often die. A massive live crocodile was reputed to have been part of the gift package (a wooden replica hangs in Seville Cathedral today). Given the lack of water on the voyage, we suspect that the semiaquatic reptile was brought as a taxidermy specimen. Likewise, instead of a live elephant, the delegation likely brought a tusk from what is known as a big tusker from sub-Saharan West Africa.

The enormous tusk still hangs today over an entrance to Seville Cathedral, next to the wooden crocodile. In the Roman period, victors like Scipio Africanus used elephant tusks as a sign of conquest. Scipio displayed 1,231 ivory tusks as part of his triumphal parade in Rome (Pliny, *Natural History* 33.53.148). In the medieval period, churches hung ivory in conspicuous places, including Lund Cathedral in Germany, Canterbury Cathedral in England, and Saint Peter's Basilica in Rome – Saint Michael's, the Romanesque church in Hildesheim,Germany, has a mammoth, not elephant, tusk (Shalem 2004: 126–127).

In the medieval period, the practice of hanging elephant tusks in churches drew largely on a crusade mentality that associated captive elephants with the elimination of Islam. The Christian princes in Europe in the medieval period had used the three live elephants as signs of victorious power over Islam. Charlemagne's elephant, not only a mark of an alliance with the 'Abbasid empire, was also a sign of his subjugation of Islam, a desire he had not achieved in failed military conflicts with the emirate of Cordoba. Frederick's elephant was dressed up in a mock-Saracen war outfit in a procession, marking a public sign of his victory of Islam in the crusades, one of his most ardent aspirations.

Figure 12 Detail of animal tribute to Alfonso X from the *Cantigas de Santa María*, no. 29. El Escorial, Spain. Author's photograph from facsimile edition.

Louis IX of France brought back an elephant as a sign of a crusade victory, even though it had failed.

Most of medieval Europe never saw the three live elephants, but, at the end of the twelfth century, an object known as an oliphant became a popular victory symbol. Produced in southern Italy under Norman hegemony, some eighty oliphants survive (Shalem 2004; Rosser-Owen 2015). An oliphant, literally Old French for "elephant," is an elephant tusk, often carved, put in metal mounts and acquired by military elites and churches. In Spain, one oliphant from the period is found in the cathedral in Zaragoza.

The production of oliphants mainly coincided with late twelfth-century historiography's desire to adopt the elephant tusk as a sign of victory over Islam. Famously referenced in the popular eponymous French medieval romance (which was also well known in early thirteenth-century Iberia), Roland blows from his oliphant as he defeats the Saracens. King Alfonso, largely responsible for converting Seville's mosques into churches, placed the elephant tusk that he received as a gift from Egypt in its cathedral, which was constructed on the former site of the city's principal mosque.

Aside from hanging the great elephant tusk, Alfonso X commissioned now-lost ivory plaques for himself to be placed in the cathedral in Seville. In 1279, Alfonso transferred the remains of the bodies of both his parents to Seville and interred them in a chapel presided over by an image of Mary. He planned that his own body should be interred in the same chapel. Alfonso's last will and testament, written in Seville in 1284, described the plaques that should be put on the high altar of that lavish chapel dedicated to Mary. He notes that they should be carried out of the chapel for processions celebrating Mary. Alfonso celebrated Mary as iconographically central to his reign, given the *Las Cantigas* book project in Mary's honor and his wife's Virxe Abrideira statuette (see Section 5). Moreover, it is noteworthy that Alfonso wrote that the panel of plaques above his sepulcher should include "many ivory images that show the stories of the deeds of Holy Mary."[31]

The practice of carving oliphants in the pre-Gothic period paled in comparison to the production of images of the Virgin Mary during the Gothic century. Miniatures from Alfonso's *Cantigas* depict images of the Virgin and Child on battle flags. One battle-scene illustration from the manuscript shows an attack on Muslim forces with the Christians holding a red flag with a white image of the Enthroned Virgin and Child (Rico Codex 240 r).

The white image of the Virgin and Child on the colored battle scene suggests that the artists who designed the fabric for the flags may have imitated statuettes in ivory of enthroned Madonnas, used by the king and his father as portable war icons. Alfonso highly cherished an elephant ivory Virgin and Child sculpture that he inherited from his father Fernando (Estela 1984). Alfonso used the legacy item, his father's ivory statuette, popularly called the Virgin of the Battles (Figure 13), to aid him in battles of Christians against Moors. The icon, carved at a workshop in Reims, was a gift from King Louis IX. The French king, who had gifted his brother-in-law the king of England with a live elephant, gifted his cousin King Ferdinand the elephant-ivory Madonna and Child.

Ferdinand and his son Alfonso considered the ivory Virgin of the Battles a talisman in the centuries-long project to Christianize Iberia against Islamic forces. In the Christian Byzantine empire, images made from elephant ivory that represented holy figures were carried as standards when troops marched into battle. One Byzantine ivory icon of Saint Demetrious found in the Cloisters at

---

[31] "una tabla grande estorial en que ha muchas imagines de marfil fechas a estorias de fechos de Santa Maria" (Torres Fuentes 2008: 345).

Figure 13 Virgin of the Battles, ca. 1240–50. Medium: ivory with gold vestiges
on hem of veil, polychrome on lips and neck. Dimensions: height 43.5 cm;
width 16.5 cm. Created in Reims. Seville Cathedral.
Open access Wikipedia Commons.

the Metropolitan Museum of Art (1970.324.3) has a cleft at the base to be inserted
on a pole to serve as a battle standard. Likewise, the Virgin of the Battles has an
indentation in the back designed to fit on the top of a horse saddle for display in
battles. One early modern source (1579) notes that when King Ferdinand's
sepulcher was moved, the ivory statuette was found because Alfonso, who had
mounted it on his horse in the conquest of the kingdom of Murcia (1243–5), had
later placed it on his father's chest before burial (Laguna Paul 2009).

A shift occurred in the thirteenth century with regards to the location of the principal ivory-producing centers on the Iberian Peninsula. In the eleventh century, the production of carvings in Cordoba – and to a lesser degree those produced in Cuenca under the patronage of Banū Dhī al-Nūn (r. 1023–80) under the Muslim Berber dynasty that reigned over the Taifa of Toledo (Marinetto Sánchez 1987) – had overshadowed the isolated production of Christian sacred images at the monastery complex of San Millán de la Cogolla (Franco Mata 2006). During Alfonso's reign, particularly after his conquest of Cordoba, Christian Castile gained hegemony over ivory production in Iberia. Christian Iberia became the peninsula's principal ivory consumer. Not only did Christian Iberia repurpose or loot Islamic ivory objects, but the output of sub-Saharan-sourced ivory at ivory-carving workshops in Alfonso's kingdom replaced the last bastions of Islamic ivory production.[32] San Millán de la Cogolla, the northern area controlled by Christian forces, which had been Iberia's ivory-producing outlier, was replaced in turn in the fourteenth century by Iberia's new ivory-producing outlier, the Nasrid dynasty that ruled the emirate of Granada (1230–1492) (Shalem 2005b; Galán y Galindo 2011; Silva Santa-Cruz 2012). In short, the margins or periphery of ivory production in fourteenth-century Iberia shifted from a region controlled by the Christians to one controlled by Muslims.

Spain under Alfonso connected elephant ivory to its Christianization project. In Iberia, religious orders had a role in military campaigns, and medieval Spanish historiography connected the conquest of the peninsula from Islam to ivory and the Virgin Mary. Rodrigo Jiménez de Rada (ca. 1170–1247), archbishop of Toledo, who led the Christian ideological charge over Muslim Iberia, described the eighth-century conquest of the Moors as led by King Rodrigo, who wore a gold crown drawn Roman-style, lying on a bed made from ivory, "as required by the protocol of the Gothic Kings" (qtd. in Rodriguez 2020: 72). Rada established the preferred Christian war image as being that of Virgin and Child. He writes that kings carry standards of the image of Mary into battle because she always was the protector and patron of Toledo and "all" Spain (Bango Torviso and López de Guereño Sanz 2009: 333).

Another reference to an ivory icon is also found in a *cantiga*, one of Alfonso's songs devoted to the Virgin Mary: a person wears a statuette of the Virgin and Child made from elephant ivory around his neck. The songs in *Las Cantigas* formed part of the most expensive and ambitious book-production project ever launched in medieval Europe. As well as being monarch of the kingdoms of

---

[32] Islamic Spain produced pommels on parade swords and pyxides (cylindrical boxes), among a vast array of other items. See Shalem 2005b; for a catalogue of Al-Andalus ivories, see Metropolitan 1993; and for women's role in ivory production in the Umayyad court, see Anderson and Rosser-Owen 2015.

Castile and León, Alfonso X was a prolific poet and, in the last two decades of his life, commissioned other poets to add to his growing corpus of songs dedicated to the Virgin Mary. The massive book project included collaborators with a variety of skills. Some were able poets who composed verses in Galician-Portuguese, the language in Alfonso's court for sung lyric poetry. It involved educated musicians, who wrote down the musical notation for the songs, and a translation team, who created a Galician-Portuguese poetic corpus out of pan-European miracles originally written in Latin and other vernaculars including the Hispano-Arabic dialect spoken in Seville. Finally, the collaborators for Alfonso's book project included visual artists or illuminators, many of whom also worked as copyists or worked closely in the scriptorium with copyists (Ferreira 2016).

One of the books that they produced is the Barbieri manuscript, and the illustration for Cantiga 299 shows the image of Alfonso complete with crown, red lips, blue tunic, and red cape.[33] An object held by the king, however, is unfinished.[34] On one side of the illustration for Cantiga 299, a group of friars from the Order of Holy Mary of Spain are kneeling, and on the other side is Queen Violante, who kneels flanked by what appear to be their children. The king looks at the barely visible icon, holding it up in his two hands. A close examination of the unfinished sketch reveals that Alfonso is holding a portable religious icon (Figure 14). One can make out a sitting figure holding another on its lap. Carefully examining the unfinished image reveals two heads and, perhaps, the arms of one figure holding the smaller one.

The illustrator of the manuscript page relied on the lyrics for Cantiga 299 in creating the image. The lyrics to this song describe a friar with an ivory pendant around his neck. The Virgin appeared to the friar in several dreams and instructed him to give the pendant to the king. After he had handed the sculpture to Alfonso, the king held it aloft and gave thanks to the Virgin. The lyrics also reveal that the icon, as we would suspect in a collection of songs devoted to Mary, is a Madonna icon.

According to the lyrics, the person "wore around his neck an image of ivory of this Lady who guides us, holding Her Son in Her arms" (Kulp-Hill 2000: 363).[35] Cantiga 299 states that the person is a member of the Order of Holy Mary. As part

---

[33] The results of the collaboration were four manuscripts containing the lyrics to approximately 419 *cantigas* or songs; musical notation for many of them; and more than 250 full-page illustrations. Of the four large thirteenth-century manuscripts of Alfonso's *Cantigas* that survive, three are in Spain in the Madrid area – one in the National Library and two in the library at the Escorial outside of Madrid. The fourth, the Barbieri manuscript, is in Florence, Italy.

[34] The image joins other illustrations in the manuscript that are not fully complete – indicating the work-in-progress nature of the manuscript. The staves that accompany Cantiga 299 are also empty, and therefore the music is not preserved, making it nearly impossible to know for certain the original music that accompanied the words.

[35] "ũa omagen desta que nos guía, d' almafí, que séu Fill' en braços ten" (Casson 2023).

Figure 14 King Alfonso holding ivory Virgin and Child, a gift from the Order of Holy Mary of Spain. *Cantigas de Santa María*, no. 299. Florence Codex, fol. 100 r. Author's photograph from facsimile edition.

of Alfonso X's connection between Mary and the Iberian military Christianization project, he founded the Order of Holy Mary of Spain (Santa María de España) in 1273, whose emblem bore an eight-pointed star with the Virgin and Child in the center (Kulp-Hill 2000: 363n.1). The Order of Holy Mary of Spain was part of the Cistercian order, a Catholic religious order of monks and nuns who connected theological doctrine with ivory. According to the Cistercians, most especially as espoused by Guerric of Igny (ca. 1080–1157), the biblical line "the king made a great throne of ivory and overlaid it with the finest gold" (1 Kings 10) connects Mary to Solomon's ivory throne. Guerric explained that Mary sits on Solomon's throne, a receptacle for God's wisdom; based on the Cistercian connection with Mary's ivory throne as sacred container, Virgin and Child statuettes were created out of ivory (Guérin 2022: 62).

The iconological significance of Madonna thrones in ivory in Alphonsin Spain (as in the Gothic period in Europe) is that Mary sits in the place of Christ, who was considered synonymous with Solomon the king. The line from the *cantiga*, "an image of ivory of this Lady who guides us," uses a specific word to denote the material and its animal origin. In specifying the material composition of statuette, the author uses *almafí*, the medieval Gallician-Portuguese word for ivory. The Spanish word *marfil* (ivory), like *almafí*, its Gallician-Portuguese semantic cousin, combines two Arabic words, '*azm* (عظم or bone) and *fíl* (فيل or elephant). The etymology indicates that those who touched it probably knew the object was a remnant of the large beast.

Most scholars would point to the illustration of Cantiga 299 as evidence that the artists of the thirteenth-century Florence manuscript did not finish coloring this picture. But the barely perceptible sketch or preparatory drawing is a cue to consider materiality. The unfinished image is a phantasmal sign. It – unintentionally – evokes the vestige of something. The fuzzy image and the word *almafi* from the manuscript are cues to wonder about the afterlife and life of an elephant: What is the unfinished image, and why was it drawn? What power does touching ivory give the king? Would the queen have an interest in holding it?

6 A Virgin and Child Statuette

So much ivory was supplied to Europe in the Middle Ages that Sarah M. Guérin (2022) calls the period from 1230–1330 the "Gothic century of ivory sculpture." One artifact from the Gothic century is a small ivory Virgin and Child sculpture made from the tusk of an African elephant that sits in a glass case in a small museum adjacent to the Monastery of Santa Clara in the town of Allariz in Galicia, Spain (Figure 15). Imagine for a moment that you are holding the ivory image. Grasping the small sculpture of Mary and Jesus, you can open and close the two hinged doors that reveal the Joys of Mary, important scenes from the Virgin's life.

In the following section, we study the history of the ivory statuette. A plausible route by which the ivory statuette arrived in Allariz is as follows: It was extracted from an elephant, whom we have named Kouyaté, in the Mali empire; carried across the Sahara on northeast trade routes to Egypt; shipped on a sea route to Majorca and then from Majorca to Cadiz, whereupon it was shipped over land to Seville. It was then carved in King Alfonso X's ivory workshop. Upon the king's death, the statuette accompanied Queen Violante on her travels until she bequeathed it to the monastery in Allariz. We created a map to show the likely route from the ivory's African origins to Galicia (Figure 16).

The likely chronology for the arrival of this statuette in Allariz can be told from the point of view of the people who touched it: A previously anonymous African elephant was born and nursed by their mother; their ivory tusk grew until they were killed; the tooth or incisor was grasped by a hunter and taken across the Sahara in a camel caravan to Egypt; it was sent to Majorca, arrived at a port in the south of Spain, and was carried by horseback to Seville. A sculptor then shaped the tusk into a silky white statuette of the Virgin and Child at a workshop, most probably in Seville. Queen Violante of Aragon carried and opened and closed the figurine. The nuns of the convent of Santa Clara did the same for centuries. Finally, the statuette was handled by art historians and conservators in the small museum where it now resides.

Figure 15 The Virxe Abrideira, ca. 1260–75, Spanish. Medium: elephant ivory, base ebony and ivory. Dimensions: height 32.5 cm; width 10 cm; depth 13.5 cm. Allariz, Spain, Monastery of Santa Clara. Photograph: David Araujo.

The Virxe (pronounced "Vir-shey") Abrideira, Galician for "Opening Virgin," is a full-relief statuette with doors that open and close on its front side. The finely sculpted details and fragile construction of the Allariz statuette suggest that it did not have a role on the battlefield like the similar ivory statuette inherited by King Alfonso from his father. Violante's statuette occupied a place of private worship.

Isidro Bango Torviso and Margarita Estella Marcos, leading art historians who have examined Violante's statuette, date the Virxe Abrideira within the Gothic century. They place its creation in the early part of the second half of the thirteenth century, a period marked by the height of Alfonso X's patronage of the arts. Both art historians estimate that, based on its style, the Virxe Abrideira was sculpted between 1260 and 1275.[36]

---

[36] Bango Torviso notes the figure among the Joys of Mary of Mary stepping on the beast dates it toward the middle rather than late thirteenth century (Bango Torviso 2010: 169). For more on date of the Virxe Abrideira, also see González Hernando 2011: 424.

Figure 16 Plausible route through which Kouyaté's tusk passed from sub-Saharan Africa to Allariz, Spain. Photograph: Avery Bonnette.

The following presents a reverse chronology of the Virxe Abrideira, that is, a history in reverse, from the location of the statuette today back to the ivory that sat inside Kouyaté's mouth. From 1993 to the present day, it has not been possible to touch the Virxe Abrideira statuette physically because it is on display in a glass case in a museum adjacent to the convent where cloistered nuns live. In 2009, the Spanish art historian Isidro Bango Torviso removed it for an exhibition in Murcia (Spain). Bango Torviso examined it closely, noting places in which ivory had been added, such as part of the throne, an insert in folds on her right knee, and one of Mary's hands.

Prior to its inclusion in the convent's museum, the Virxe Abrideira was a devotional object in the Clarissa convent for about 800 years (most likely from 1301 to 1993). Archival evidence confirms that it did not leave the possession of the nuns in the Allariz monastery for six centuries, and, if its thirteenth century dating is confirmed, it most probably did not leave their possession for eight.[37] The survival of the statuette in northwest Spain is nothing short of remarkable. It survived possible looting, damage in war, and destruction in religious prohibitions.[38] The isolation of the remote town of Allariz and its cloistered residents no doubt played a role in its preservation.

The sacred medieval ivory statuette was not kept in a case but handled by the cloistered Clarissa nuns. Some enthroned Virgin and Child sculptures have interior cavities fitted as reliquaries or pyxides for the Eucharist, making those Marian statuettes symbolic icons of the bearer of God (Guérin 2022: 80). In the case of the Virxe Abrideira, instead of a Eucharist or relic, the tabernacle opens to reveal the Joys of Mary, which take place under pointed Gothic arches in the form of a clover.

The nuns took a special interest in the hinged shrine on holy occasions. The interior scenes of the statuette, the depiction of the vignettes of the Joys of the Virgin, was commonly celebrated in literature written in the Spanish vernacular of the period.[39] The scenes on the interior of the statuette read continuously across the three leaves and from bottom to top, culminating in the Coronation of the Virgin. Identifiable on the central lower panel is the Nativity, then above it is the Assumption, and finally above that is the Coronation. The devotional value of the statuette was appreciated on the corresponding feast days of the Joys, such as the Annunciation (March 25, the commemoration of the day when the angel Gabriel informed Mary she would be the mother of Jesus Christ) or Assumption (August 15, the holy day that marks the Virgin's bodily ascent to heaven).

The nuns would have regarded Mary as an intercessor of divine proportions and an intimate guide who intervened in everyday affairs. Images of Mary were omnipresent in Alfonsin Spain. They were not only carried into battle but also

---

[37] The first archival documents that describe the Virxe Abrideira in the monastery in Allariz are from the sixteenth century. They include a list of objects in the monastery written in 1567; a firsthand account by Ambrosio de Morales, who went to Galicia in 1572; and an account from a historian of the province of Santiago, Fray Jacobo de Castro (d. 1735) (Bango Torviso 2010: 140–141; Bango Torviso and López de Guereño Sanz 2009: 346; Estela Marcos 1984: 131–132).

[38] With regards to religious prohibition, the statuette could have been destroyed in the late Middle Ages, when people such as the chancellor of the University of Paris and religious reformer Jean Gerson (1363–1429) prohibited the representation of sacred scenes in Mary's womb (Bango Torviso and López de Guereño Sanz 2009: 342). Later, more icon destruction occurred during the Spanish Counter-reformation, when, for example, statues of the pregnant Madonna were destroyed (Beusterien 2020a).

[39] Two passages dedicated to the Joys are found in Alfonso X's *Cantigas*. Other passages dedicated to the Joys are found in different vernacular works such as in the section "Milagro galardón de la Virgen" (The Virgin's Miracle Gift) in the *Milagros de Nuestra Señora* (The Miracles of Our Lady) by Gonzalo de Berceo (1195–1294) and in the *Libro de buen amor* (Book of Good Love) by the Arcipreste de Hita (fourteenth century). For histories of the cult to Mary in medieval Spain, see Gerli's introduction to Berceo (1989) and Salvador Martínez 2010.

erected at the entrance to towns and put up at roadsides. They were in private chapels, or – as was the case of the Virxe Abrideira – they *were* private chapels. The cult of Mary occupied not just feast days but sensorial life in thirteenth-century Spain. The songs from Alfonso's *Cantigas* are replete with stories of animated virgins. Virgin statues speak (25, 87, 303); become angry and shout (164); and cry tears (59); and their breasts give milk (46) (Pittaway 2018). The interior scenes of the statuette could be touched, as well as the figure of the Virgin and Child when closed. As the popular songs of the *Cantigas* attest, Marian statues were devotional objects in the sense that they were avatars of Mary herself, overcoming trials, helping to cope with suffering, and curing illnesses.

Miniatures from manuscripts of Saint Hedwig's life indicate the intimacy of worship between women and portable statuettes in Europe in the Middle Ages (Figure 17). In her study of shrine Madonna icons that open and close, art historian Elena Gertzman underscores that prayer practice did not only involve observation from a distance. It involved touching and play. The ivory statuette of the Virgin and Child depicted in the pages of Saint Hedwig's vita gained living agency when she turned it "every which way" in her hands and held it out to be touched or kissed by those in need of cure (Gertzman 2020: 223 and 2015; Jung 2010; and Schleif 2009).

The Virxe Abrideira opened and closed. It concealed and revealed. As an object of wonder, the Galician ivory statuette gained agency in the hands of the nuns who lived in the Clarissa monastery. One ivory statue of the Virgin and Child from the same period as the Virxe Abrideira shows a seated Mary with Child and a cradle on her lap (Figure 18). Nuns were given cradles to cultivate devotion for the Christ Child, often prompting visions of personal encounters with him. In a similar fashion, the smooth ivory statue of the Allariz Virgin and Child most likely was also held close to one's body like a doll, a puppy, or rosary beads.

White, satiny, and warm when held, the haptic experience for the nuns in the monastery in Galicia included carrying, opening, probing, and stroking. At different times for different nuns, the statuette meant different things. Ivory, for instance, was connected to chastity. Sarah Guérin (2022: 80) notes that the theme of chastity and the body as receptacle was a recurring topos in thirteenth-century ivory sculptures of Mary. Bede the Venerable (ca. 672/3–735) paid special attention to the connection between ivory and chastity. Bede interprets the biblical verse "His belly is as of ivory" (Song of Songs 5:14) as connected to chastity: "Ivory properly signifies chastity, which remains immune in the flesh from the corruption of the sins of the flesh" (qtd. in Guérin 2022: 156).[40] The

---

[40] Bede's original reads: "Ebur decorum castitatis, qua a corruptione peccati carnis immune permansit, indicat." Herbert L. Kessler offers an alternative translation: "Ivory indicates the

Figure 17 Saint Hedwig holding an ivory statuette with nun kissing it. Hedwig Codex, Silesia, 1353, fol. 46 v, detail. Los Angeles, J. Paul Getty Museum, MS Ludwig XI.7 (83.MN126). Photo: Courtesy of J. Paul Getty Museum Open Content Program.

sermon on the Annunciation by Guerric of Igny states: "I prefer now to wonder at that ivory of virginal chastity, so precious or rather priceless" (qtd. in Guérin 2022: 75).

Some regarded the ivory Virgin as the epitome of beauty, inspired by classical sculpture with enveloped folds in the drapery that lyrically veil a body that generates a sense of life within. The substance itself was a beauty standard. When Anna Komnene (1083–1153), Greek historian and daughter of the Byzantine emperor Alexios I Komnenos (r. 1081–1118), described the grace

---

splendor of chastity through which, while in the Flesh, he remained free of the corruption of the flesh" (Kessler 2015: 72).

Figure 18 Virgin and Child with cradle, ca. 1350–1400, German, ivory, traces
of polychromy, 31.5 × 12.8 × 8.5 cm. Metropolitan Museum of Art, New York,
accession number: 17.190.182. Open access CC0.

of her mother's gestures and hands in *The Alexiad*, she did so through an ivory
metaphor: "from the shape of her hands and fingers you would have thought that
they were wrought in ivory by some artificer" (Dawes 1928).

Some nuns would have noticed that the artists left the faces unpainted on the
human figures on the Virxe statuette. For the artistic mediums of carved marble
or illuminated parchment, the color of the material became the skin color of the
skin of the sacred figure. All sacred images with white faces were significant in
shaping modes of thought related to white skin, but ivory, because of its prestige
and value, played an especially significant role in establishing ivory whiteness
as a beauty standard. Color had *not* been applied to the face of the Virxe

statuette, so ivory whiteness became the paragon hue of whiteness for skin color, a model that impacted the self-invention of the category of whiteness not just for the nuns, but for Europe writ large.[41]

Aside from symbolizing chastity or the ivory color of a beautiful face, the ivory of the statuette connected to Mary's status as king. As mentioned, the Order of Holy Mary of Spain, part of the Cistercian order and founded in Alfonsin Spain, connected the Virgin with Solomon's ivory seat. The biblical Throne of Wisdom (*sedes sapientiae*) was the typological referent depicted at the start of the Gothic century of ivory (Guérin 2022: 61). In the case of the Galician statuette, additional ivory was used to create the throne (Figure 19). The image of the seated Mary symbolized kingliness for some nuns because Mary sits in the place of Christ as the equivalent of Solomon the king. A sermon, probably composed by Nicholas of Clairvaux (d. 1178), describes the connection between the ivory of Solomon's throne and Mary.[42] The sermon glosses the biblical line about Solomon's throne by stating that ivory is characterized by brightness and strength, both of which are connected to Mary's virginity because she shines in radiance and was chosen for her strength (Iafrate 2015: 242). References to ivory and Solomon's Song of Songs also may have served to develop the growing self-invention connected to an ivory-white skin complexion. The Song of Songs describes the beloved's neck as like an ivory tower, and commentaries such as that of Saint Jerome interpret "I am black, *and/but* beautiful" (*nigra sum, sed formosa*) as a miraculous change in complexion, from black to white, as from black to beauty, and sin to purity (T. Flanigan, pers. comm., 2024).

Some nuns also would have also connected the material of the statuette with elephants. The gap between recognizing ivory and its source varied between individuals and cultures. Early on, however, many nuns in Alfonsin Spain spoke Arabic or a Hispano-Arabic dialect, and they would have recognized the elephant behind the material because the root Arabic word *fīl* (elephant) is part and parcel of Iberian Latinate words for ivory, *almafi* (Gallician-Portuguese) and *marfil* (Spanish). For many, the words elephant and ivory were the same thing. Two late medieval writers, the Castilian poet Alfonso Álvarez de Villasandino (ca. 1340–ca. 1424) and Ruy González de Clavijo

---

[41] Several scholars have pointed out the connection between ivory whiteness and race. For further discussion of the self-invention of the category of whiteness in the mid-thirteenth century, see Caviness 2008. For race in medieval Iberia, see Patton 2022. For race in the *Cantigas*, see Patton 2016. For the connection between ivory sculptures and an artificial whiteness belonging to the skin of holy bodies, see Bleeke 2020 and McCracken 2020. For the racial valence of the dark skin color of Virgins in the early modern period, see Beusterien 2020a.

[42] The authorship of *Sermo in nativitate beatae Mariae virginis* (Sermon on the Birth of the Holy Virgin Mary) is often erroneously ascribed to Peter Damian (Iafrate 2015: 242).

Figure 19 Reverse view of Virxe Abrideira with Throne of Wisdom. Virxe
Abrideira, ca. 1260–75, Spanish. Medium: elephant ivory, base ebony and
ivory. Dimensions: height 32.5 cm; width 10 cm; depth 13.5 cm. Allariz, Spain,
Monastery of Santa Clara. Photograph by John Beusterien.

(Castilian author, traveler, and chamberlain to the king, d. 1412), conflated the
words *marfil* (ivory) and *elefante* (elephant) (Dutton and Cuenca 1993: 246;
Clavijo 1782: 172–177).[43]

---

[43] By the early modern period, most writers distinguished between *marfil* and elephant, but some,
such as the Portuguese physician Garcia de Orta, were aware of the Arabic derivation of *-fil* (Orta
1563: 84). Thanks to Abel Alves for references.

Those in the monastery that recognized "elephant bone" in the word ivory would have, in the same way that a bone of a saint was metonymic of the holy person, understood that the material harbored the essence of the large, exotic beast. The haptic experience of the statuette, then, brought the remnant of the elephant closer, like the remnant of a holy saint. The connection with *fīl* for some may have evoked classical sources that claimed that elephants had cold blood and that the elephants themselves, like their ivory, were considered chaste animals (Guérin 2022: 76–77). Nicholas of Clairvaux's sermon about the Solomon throne mentions that ivory has a cold quality, connecting it with the belief in the relative coldness of women's bodies (Paster 1998). English theologian Alexander Neckam (1157–1217) writes in *De naturis rerum* (On the Nature of Things): "observe how chaste an animal the elephant is and how cold by nature … even ivory, which is the elephant's bone, is in holy writ a symbol of chastity" (qtd. Druce 1919: 40–41). In the cool stone chambers of the Galician monastery, the nuns who touched the statuette might have connected not only the object with iconographic symbolisms of humoral coldness in women and elephants, but the experience of touching the ivory itself. When first felt, the ivory statuette was cold, but in one's hands or close to the body it became warm.

Although the evidence is not conclusive, the Virxe Abrideira was most likely bequeathed to the monastery by Queen Violante. Prior to its 800-year history inside the monastery, the queen carried the icon as part of her private entourage during the last quarter of the thirteenth century. Instead of remaining in one place, we suspect it moved with her as one of the objects in her traveling private chapel (neither King Alfonso nor, in her later role as dowager, Queen Violante had a permanent palace). Violante survived her husband by seventeen years, and evidence suggests that she kept the Allariz statuette after his death. The best evidence that the statuette belonged to Violante is found in historical documents relating to the Convent of the Clarissas. The queen founded the convent of Santa Clara de Allariz, the first mendicant institution to be endowed by a member of the Castilian royal family (Katz 2009: 55). In her will, dated 1292, the dowager Violante instructed that her remains, and all worldly goods, be left to the convent – "and I leave them [the nuns at the Clarissa monastery] all of my chapel, all that I have with me as well as all that I have already given" (qtd. in Katz 2012: 93)[44] – and the Virxe Abrideira formed part of her chapel of private

---

[44] "et mandolas toda mi capiela, assi lo que yo di como lo que yo tengo" (qtd. Bango Torviso and López de Guereño Sanz 2009: 346). Violante's choice of Galicia for her remains needs study. On the one hand, in an act of separation from her husband, she chose a different burial institution for her remains, but, on the other, she chose Galicia, a region favored by the king. Today, the location of Violante's remains is unknown.

devotion. Today, besides the Virxe Abrideira, several other thirteenth-century objects from Violante's private chapel are found in the museum adjacent to the convent.

Violante played a significant role in the royal marriage. She acted as political diplomat for the king in critical negotiations related to her husband's military campaigns with members of the Islamic faith in the bordering kingdom of Granada, as well as in North Africa. She also created an alliance through marriage for Alfonso's kingdoms of Castile and León with the kingdom of Aragon, because her father was the king of Aragon.

Since the Virxe Abrideira is estimated to have been carved around the late 1260s or early 1270s (p. 63), Queen Violante might have played role in the patronage of the Allariz statuette because during the period before 1270, her personal funds had not yet been cut off (Katz 2009). It was not unusual for elite women to commission ivory. One of Violante's contemporaries in England is recorded as having bought ivory. A household expense account from 1251–3 for Eleanor of Provence (1223–91) records the purchase of 1.6 kilograms of ivory to make images (Guérin 2022: 178). But it is more likely that, instead of purchasing the ivory, the raw material had been gift from Violante's father, because he controlled the island of Majorca, the principal supplier of ivory to Europe during the Gothic century.

One miniature from the *Cantigas* provides visual evidence of Queen Violante's intimate worship when the statuette was in her possession. The image shows a prostrate Violante in front of a Virgin and Child statuette (Figure 20). No written account describes Violante's interaction with the ivory statuette. Nonetheless, a text dedicated to the Joys of the Virgin belonging to Yolande de Soissons, a French worshipper, indicates how not only the nuns after her, but also Violante may have practiced worship in front of the Virxe. Yolande's verbal instructions describe action taken during prayer: "I will kneel down in front of your image fifteen times and honour it in memory of the fifteen joys you had of your true son on Earth" (qtd. in Guérin 2022: 175). Violante may have not only knelt in front of the ivory statuette but may also have sung her prayers to the icon. The first song in Alfonso's *Cantigas* begins by celebrating the seven joys: "This is the first song of praise to Holy Mary, enumerating the seven Joys She had from Her Son" (Kulp-Hill 2000: 3).[45] Alfonso's song of the Joys of Mary therefore also corresponds to the images of the Joys of Mary that are found on the interior panels of the ivory statuette.

---

[45] "Esta é a primeira cantiga de loor de Santa María, ementando os séte goios que houve de séu Fillo" (Casson 2023).

Figure 20 Violante prostrated before Virgin and Child, *Cantigas de Santa María*, Florence Codex, fol. 8 r. Author's photograph from facsimile edition.

Moving back further in the story of the statuette, the Virxe Abrideira was not designed as an object to be carried into battle, as it is a portable chapel with delicate details and figurines of prophets that once stood on its base. It has no slot like the Virgin of the Battles that could be fitted on a saddle. It was designed by artists in a workshop in the kingdom of Castile, controlled by the king. Toledo was one location of Alfonso's itinerant court, but Seville is the most likely candidate for the location of the ivory workshop where the sculpture was made. Multiple historical facts support the conclusion that Alfonso would have chosen a Seville workshop for the sculpting of the Virxe Abrideira: the king had converted Seville's mosques into churches and commissioned an ivory altar for its cathedral; he buried his father in the Cathedral of Seville with the ivory statuette of the Virgin of the Battles; and he composed the praise *Cantigas* to Mary while he resided in Seville, specifically in the Gothic Palace in the Royal Alcázar, the location of the scriptorium where he oversaw the book's production.

Whereas Alfonso's father received the Virgin of the Battles as a gift from France, Alfonso commissioned his own ivory works. The ivory used for the statuette probably arrived at the workshop in the late 1260s, shortly before it was presented to Violante. Skilled anonymous artists who handled the tusk first created a prototype of the shape of the Madonna and Child statue, the Salamanca Shrine Madonna and Child, found today in the Cathedral of Salamanca in the old Chapter room of the Cloisters (Figure 21). It has the same dimensions from the open neck to feet as the Virxe Abrideira statuette.[46] The prototype, however, is made from lesser-quality materials. The artists used wood and marble, not ivory, to shape the maquette in a test of the innovative form of the statue.

Just as a team of collaborators produced books under Alfonso X's patronage, a team of artists worked on the ivory statuette and its marble prototype. A depiction of a workshop in *The Book about Chess, Dice and Board Games* (*Libro del ajedrez, dados y tablas*), produced under Alfonso's patronage, depicts how a team of skilled artists worked in collaboration in producing ivory products (Guérin 2022: 27–28). Not only was the ivory commissioned, but also material to make paints. One job the team carried out was to create the paints, just as they did for images of Mary, whether carved from stone, wood, or ivory. One illustration from *Las Cantigas* shows the creation and application of blue paint to a Marian icon (Figure 22).

Artists added paint to the prototype and the ivory statuette, following Gothic models found in Iberia and throughout Europe. French curator and art historian Danielle Gaborit-Chopin (1997) notes that, when paint was applied to ivory Virgin and Child sculptures in the second half of the thirteenth century, it was done so in small touches with great restraint. Blue paint on the Virxe Abrideira, the traditional color of the virgin, has been added to the interior of Mary's veil. In the interior scenes of the statuette, blue paint was added to God and to Mary's eyes. Aside from the paint, the team created gold leaf. In the tiny images in the panel of the statuette in which God crowns Mary, gold leaf still exists on the thrones, collars, and crowns of God and Mary.

Traces of blue or red paint in the interior panels of the Virxe Abrideira suggest that color was only added to select features on the face such as the lips and eyes, just like they are on the Salamanca prototype. The materiality of the prototype and the finished product are significant with regard to the history of whiteness. As already noted (p. 68–69), the faces were left unpainted. The absence of paint on the face of the final version of the statuette, rather than paint itself, highlights the artist's skin-color preferences. The artists, aware of variations of shades of

---

[46] Bango Torviso writes "Que es hispana, no tengo duda al igual que pertenecen a un mismo taller (de la de Salamanca)" (I have no doubt that it is of Spanish origins, just as I am certain it was created in the same workshop as the Salamanca Virgin) (pers. comm., November 10, 2021). He further notes that the Salamanca statuette confirms the dating of the Allariz sculpture prior to 1275, because an inventory item indicates that the statuette of the Virgin and Child had already arrived in the sanctuary in the Cathedral of Salamanca in 1275.

Figure 21 Salamanca Shrine Madonna and Child, ca. 1260–75, Spanish. Medium: wood and marble with gilding and polychromy; missing five scenes out of six in the wings; lower scene in the center panel; nine out of eleven prophets featured on octagonal base. Dimensions: height 39 cm; width 19 cm; depth 15 cm. Las Antiguas Salas Capitulares, del Claustro de la Catedral Vieja de Salamanca, Salamanca, Spain. Wikimedia Commons.

white to black for skin complexion, left the face of the Virgin, the Child, and other holy figures unpainted, for both statuettes. The marble prototype was considered an inferior first try and the Virxe the final finished product. Given the aesthetic hierarchy, artists thereby privileged ivory over marble-white skin.

Several styles and practices from different traditions cross-fertilized in the making of the Virxe. Many members of the Alfonsin team of artists learned their trade influenced by Islamic traditions in Spain and North Africa. The artists

Figure 22 Finishing a sculpture with a coat of paint, with a helper who prepares colors at a table. Illustration from *Cantigas de Santa María*, no. 136, Codex Rico, Biblioteca del Real Monasterio de El Escorial. Author's photograph from facsimile edition.

were also familiar with Gothic sculptural styles. The styles from France, Germany, England, and Aragon entered Castilian Iberia through the enhanced intercultural exchange of ecclesiastical art along the French route to Santiago, the pilgrimage route that crossed the northern part of Iberia and ended in the city that contained the reputed relics of Saint James.

Most of the manuscripts produced by Alfonso were written in Castilian, including the books that recorded the laws for the kingdom and its history, whose authorship is also attributed to King Alfonso. But Alfonso celebrated popular styles in *Las Cantigas*, the collection of devotion hymns to Mary, by following the literary tradition of imitating the dialect from northwest Iberia, Gallician-Portuguese, for sung verse. Even though the language of the books was from the northwest part of Iberia, the poems celebrating Mary in Gallician-Portuguese were produced in Toledo and Seville, an area of Iberia where dialects of Castilian were spoken. In this way, the artists that produce *Las Cantigas* infuse a regional style in the manuscripts that contrasts with Alfonso's other manuscripts.

The Alfonsin artists who shaped the Virxe Allariz statuette also incorporated regional styles, many found in cities on the pilgrimage route to Santiago. Art historian Margarita Estella Marcos points to the disproportionately large Eucharistic doves on the Virxe Abrideira as indicative of Iberian interpretations of a Gothic theme not found in French models (Estella Marcos 1984: 133–134; Katz 2009: 86n.18). Isidro Bango Torviso notes several uniquely Iberian Gothic sculpting styles in the Marian figure that are also characteristic of ecclesiastical sculptures from the northern Spanish cities of Burgos and León, both key resting spots on the pilgrimage route. Bango Torviso also notes that features from the Salamanca prototype, like the inclusion of the prophet figures at the base, confirm the statuette's Castilian provenance.[47] Bango notes, based on the prototype, that the Allariz statuette had several small statuettes of prophets probably standing on the ebony and ivory base, and the prophets at the base form part of a uniquely Gothic iconography seen, for instance, on the West Door of the Collegiate church of Santa Maria la Mayor in Toro in the province of Zamora (Bango Torviso 2010: 181).

The team of Alphonsin artists that created the Virxe did something remarkable in the tradition of Gothic sculpture. They combined two styles, the block and hinged tabernacle, into one. Block-style ivory statuettes were ubiquitous in the Gothic century of ivory.[48] Thirteenth-century artists regularly depicted a solid block image of a triumphal Mother Mary sitting on the Throne of Wisdom and stepping on a little beast with her left foot. Examples were found throughout Europe. The Casa de Ceas, found in León, a resting place for pilgrims on the Camino of Santiago, contains one of the many examples of an ivory enthroned virgin in the whole-block style.

Though not as common as the block style, the practice of crafting hinged tabernacles was also a widespread Gothic sculptural practice. Numerous hinged tabernacles with a seated Virgin and Child were sculpted from elephant ivory, such as the Polyptych with the Madonna and Child and Scenes from the Life of Christ in the Metropolitan Museum of Art (Figure 23). Another hinged tabernacle, a triptych altar that opens with each segment shaped into a rectangle, is

---

[47] The figures have prophet attributes of the Gothic period such as tonsured hair, beards, and conical hats. They carry what seem to be phylacteries, that is, small boxes that contained sacred Hebrew texts, another common iconographic practice of the period.

[48] Examples include the enthroned Virgin and Child in the Victoria and Albert Museum, and the seated Virgin and Child found today in the Hamburg Museum für Kunst und Gewerbe. Block statues of the seated virgin were also made of other materials such as marble, including one (ca. 1330–40, Cleveland Museum of Art) by Andrés Pisano (1290–1348) and another (ca. 1364, Gulbenkian) by Jean de Liège (ca. 1330–81). Some existing ivory Virgin and Mary block statues may have been part of a larger hinged ivory tabernacles, such as the Virgin and Child ivory in the Cloisters Collection (Barnet 1997: 183). For ivory block style, see Paul Williamson in Barnet 1997: 148–149 and Guérin 2022.

Figure 23 Tabernacle polyptych with the Madonna and Child and scenes from
the life of Christ, ca. 1275–1300, northern France (?). Medium: ivory with
traces of original gilding and polychromy; silver hinges. Dimensions: height
9.7 cm; width 13.1 cm (with open wings). New York, Metropolitan Museum of
Art, Robert Lehman Collection, accession number: 1975.1.1553.
Open access CC0.

found on the pilgrim route to Santiago, in the small town of Castildelgado in the
province of Burgos. The Castildelgado altarpiece is made from wood, not ivory,
and opens to reveal an image of Mary holding Jesus, flanked by religious scenes.

The style of the Virxe Abrideira resembles that of block-style statues because
the sculpture is shaped in the form of an Enthroned Virgin and Child. It diverges
from the block style, however, because it is not solid. The interior is hollowed out.
In turn, the artists who created the Virxe Abrideira were keenly aware of hinged
tabernacles that open to reveal holy scenes within. The Allariz statuette is distinct
from other tabernacles that open and close because it is not in the shape of
a typical rectangular altar piece. The hinged tabernacle itself is the shape of the
Virgin and Child. The Alfonsin artists, therefore, fused the individual block and
hinged styles into one, creating a singularly unique Gothic work of art.[49]

---

[49] The Virxe Abrideira may be the first Virgin and Child ivory statue that opens. One in walnut wood (ca.
1240) was found in the royal abbey of Maubuisson near Paris. Another is listed in a 1343 inventory
from Notre-Dame in Paris: an ivory Virgin and Child "cut down the middle with images carved in the
opening" (qtd. in Guérin 2022: 151). A later example from the fourteenth century is found in Evora

The team would have selected a curved ivory piece that stood out in a batch of ivory because of its milky white texture and the ease with which it could be shaped. The sculptors discarded a significant portion of the tusk. Because it is too soft, experienced carvers generally remove the nerve pulp from the wide end that once sat in the bone socket. The back of the Christ Enthroned at Dumbarton Oaks Museum in Washington, DC – an elephant ivory mandorla (almond-shaped frame surrounding Christ on a throne) – provides a visual example of the inside part of the tusk that was removed (Figure 24). The Dumbarton Oaks Enthroned Christ was created out of a tusk carved for the new monastery church of San Millán de la Cogolla about 200 years before the Virxe Abrideira. If one removes the mandorla, the frame that surrounds the enthroned Christ, and examines the back of the image, a cavity in the ivory is revealed (Figure 25). This cavity once held the pulp material, which is soft and unsuitable for fine carving because it holds the newest deposits channeled through the tusk's vascular system.

After the material was removed from the pulp cavity, the conical-shaped hollow occupying 20 to 30 percent of the tusk, the artists would also have shaved away the enamel-like bark, called cementum, that covers the whiter and more satiny dentine tissue on the inside. The outermost layer of the husk and the tip of the tusk do not serve the carver because they are too brittle. The tool used to clean the exterior layer probably resembled a billhook, a tool with a sharp, curved blade for shaving away the unusable part of the tusk (a similar tool was used, ironically, to tame Asian elephants) (Guérin 2022: 27). The cementum-removal process took place before sculpting the dentine began.

Carvers generally discarded this drier material, but the Virxe Abrideira is extraordinary because it still preserves a segment of the tusk (Figure 26). The statuette sits upon a base that is made up of alternating pieces of ebony and ivory in the Andalusian style (further evidence that the statuette was sculpted in Seville). Underneath this base, part of an elephant tusk sits on another base of alternating pieces of ebony and ivory. Of over 5,000 sculpted pieces in the catalogue created by the Gothic Ivories Project from the Courtauld Institute of Arts, the small statuette from Allariz is the only one that integrates a tusk

---

Cathedral in Portugal. In later centuries, several forgeries to satisfy collectors were produced in moments of Gothic revival. Richard H. Randall notes that four such Virgin and Child sculptures (found in the Musée du Louvre, at the Musée des Beaux-Arts, Lyons, at the Musée des Antiquités, Rouen, and at the Walter Art Gallery, Baltimore) were meant to meet the demand for Gothic ecclesiastic art. Carbon dating of the forgery from the Walter Art Gallery (71.152) demonstrates that the artist (possibly from France in the eighteenth century) repurposed elephant ivory from an older ornament from 1020–1220 CE to create an attractive piece for collectors (Barnet 1997: 285–289) Another hinged tabernacle made of elephant ivory, bone, and wood inlay at the Cranbrook Art Museum (CAM 1922.2), depicting the Virgin in Glory, was purchased in Granada, Spain (Barnet 1997: 295–296). For a history of this type of sculpture, see González Hernández 2011, especially the Joys of Mary shrines (*Abrideras de gozo*) section.

Figure 24 Mandorla with Christ Enthroned, 1060–80, Spanish. Medium: elephant ivory on wood. Dimensions: height 22.7 cm; width 10.5 cm. Washington, DC, Dumbarton Oaks. Accession number BZ.1948.12. © Dumbarton Oaks, Byzantine Collection, Washington, DC.

segment as part of the sculpture. In between the lower base of alternating ebony and ivory plaques, now-lost prophet figures probably sat. The visible part of the tusk explicitly signals its elephant origin. Is short, the Virxe Abrideira incorporates a sample of the material that once surrounded the silky white ivory, making the uncrafted tusk part of the overall iconography of the sculpture.

With the inner pulp removed and the outmost layer stripped away, the grafting of the ivory statuette out of the soft material adjacent to the pulp cavity began. The ivory carver took a single block of ivory and first cut two different pieces from the

Figure 25 Nerve cavity seen on the reverse of mandorla with Christ Enthroned, 1060–80, Spanish. Medium: elephant ivory on wood. Dimensions: height 22.7 cm; width 10.5 cm. Washington, DC, Dumbarton Oaks. Accession number BZ.1948.12. © Dumbarton Oaks, Byzantine Collection, Washington, DC.

block of the tusk. One piece would comprise the Virgin's face and the miniature scenes from her life history, and the second piece of the tusk was crafted into her body up to the shoulder blades and the Christ child. This second ivory piece of the Virgin body was then cut down the middle. The artist who worked on the delicate statue used a variety of fine chisels, picks, and drills. The principal figure, the seated Virgin, was shaped by cutting perpendicular to the ground. The tiny figures carved in three-quarter relief on the sides, which suggest small free-standing sculptures, were produced through a more challenging technique in which the ivory material behind the forms was cut to leave an oblique space behind the independent figures that stand in front of the panel.

The sculptor took advantage of the natural morphology of the tooth, sculpting the dense layer of dentine, the main part of the tusk, which, when polished, produced a silky whiteness. As with many medieval ecclesiastical ivories, one

Figure 26 Detail of tusk base of Virxe Abrideira, ca. 1260–1275, Spanish.
Medium: elephant ivory, base ebony and ivory. Dimensions: height 32.5 cm;
width 10 cm; depth 13.5 cm. Allariz, Spain, Monastery of Santa Clara.
Photograph by John Beusterien.

notes the characteristic curve – the artist followed the grain, that is, the length of
the tusk. The sculptor exploited the tusk's natural curvature to create a Virgin
inclining toward her son. Three primary ivory pieces comprise the statuette –
one forms Mary's face and body, and the other was cut into two pieces that were
opened and closed, connected to the first piece by hinges. Other pieces of ivory
were added for the miniature figures and other parts of the sculpture.

Prior to arriving at Alfonso's ivory workshop in the late 1260s, someone would
have carried Kouyaté's tusk by horseback to Seville from a city on the southern
coast such as Cadiz. The Cadiz route to Seville was a key axis of merchant traffic
during Alfonso's reign, and it was a primary economic port on Mediterranean
maritime routes through which commodities arrived in Seville (Medina 2023).
One medieval icon – itself is made of ivory and originally located at San Millán de
la Cogolla – shows a possible scenario for the transportation of Kouyaté's tusk
from the southern coast of Iberia. The image depicts a group of men on horse-
sgrasping a large tusk with their hands. This image does not depict the arrival of
ivory in Seville, but it nonetheless shows one way that ivory traveled over land:
acquired elephant ivory tusks were carried by horseback to their destination.

The tusk arrived in the cargo of a vessel known as a *tarida*, which had set sail from
Majorca. The *tarida*, an Aragonese word of Arabic origin meaning any boat loaded
with cargo, was an oar-powered galley that carried the cargo that left Majorca. These
boats were capable of shipping massive loads of up to 45,400–68,000 kilograms.
Cargos also included gold, perfumes, and indigo-dyed cotton, as well as other

minerals and dyes like alum needed by the textile industry (Guérin 2015b: 38; Guérin 2022: 21). They traded in products extracted from animals such as ostrich feathers and various types of leather and hides, such as leopard skins and shields made from oryx skins. They also shipped live animals like parrots (Guérin 2022: 20). Archival thirteenth-century war documents further indicate the oar-powered *taridas* not only contained commercial goods for trade, but also other items for war, including live horses, along with their soldiers (Instituto de Historia y Cultura Naval 2016).

Majorca under King James I, a major supplier of thirteenth-century ivory to Europe, is the most likely candidate as the source for ivory sent to Alfonso X. Alfonso's load of ivory most likely left from Majorca, because King James I of Aragon acted as an intermediary in the supply route between sub-Saharan Africa and Christian Europe. After he seized the Balearic Islands in 1229 and 1231, in 1247 Queen Violante's father invited Jewish merchants fleeing Almohad Sijilmasa, the Moroccan trade entrepôt at the northern edge of the Sahara, to settle in Majorca, a principal seaport for the Aragon empire. In creating a haven for the merchants, King James acquired generations of experience in trans-Saharan trade (Guérin 2022: 21).

The material most probably was received in Majorca from a port city like Alexandria, where it had previously been shipped through the Sahara Desert in trade caravans. It is likely that the ivory followed a similar route that Mansa Mūsā I took from Timbuktu in the Mali empire through Egypt for the Hajj to Mecca. Before being shipped to Majorca, the ivory was probably carried through the deserts by caravans controlled by Imazighen (Berber) traders.[50] The load of ivory from African elephants that eventually supplied the material for the Virxe Abrideira might have also included the ebony used for the sculpture. The ebony on Violante's statuette, like the ivory, was sourced from the sub-Sahara.[51] Gabon ebony (*Diospyros crassiflora*), a dense black hardwood with a long history of serving ornamental purposes, was extracted from West Africa and shipped to Europe in the thirteenth century.

The elephant that provided the ivory died because of a hunt possibly around 1260, when they were somewhere between the ages of twenty and sixty. The person who handled Kouyaté's horn likely neither tipped it (removed it while alive) nor found it on the ground. Tusks from dead animals are rarely extracted in the savannah because by the time one might happen upon an elephant carcass, the tusk has dried out and withered and transformed into an object closer to a flaking stick unsuitable for carving.

---

[50] See back flap of Bickford Berzock (2019) for potential routes from Mali Empire to Egypt.
[51] Today, because of unsustainable harvesting, indigenous African ebony is threatened.

A likely place where Kouyaté could have been killed was within the area controlled by the Mali empire. Muslim scholar Yahyā al Zuhrī (767–856) noted as far back as the ninth century that the people in the Mali region "take many elephants by hunting and eat their flesh, then export their tusks to Egypt and Syria" (qtd. in Levtzion and Hopkins 1981: 97). If multiple elephants were killed, some of the ivory might have been processed locally. In the case of a region south of the Mali empire (in the central Zaire basin), chiefs generally held hunting rights over their territories, and they were entitled to a portion of every animal killed. For instance, Liuba chiefs received both tusks and left the hunters with only the meat (Harms 1981: 41). Giving further evidence of elephant hunting in the region, archeological digs reveal that many in small towns in thirteenth-century Mali not only hunted elephants for export markets but also used their ivory locally for personal adornment (in the form of bangles and bracelets) as a sign of elite status (Guérin 2019).

Hunters extracted Kouyaté's tusks and carried them over their shoulders across land and rivers to a trading post.[52] Although anthropologist Robert W. Harms studies the ivory trade in a later period (from 1500–1891), his description of the practice of elephant hunting in sub-Saharan Africa illustrates several possible scenarios that could describe Kouyaté's death. Harms notes that the practice in the central Zaire basin has changed little over the centuries. Descriptions of hunts indicate that 300–400 spears could have been thrust into the elephant's body. Hunters could also have smeared their bodies with odorous plants to cloak their human smell and then slipped under the animal's belly and slit a motor nerve in their leg so the animal could not run. Sometimes platforms were placed in trees, and heavy logs with spears attached would swing between two trees into the animal's body. Spears might also be placed in the animal's path or put in a large pit covered with sticks (Harms 1981: 41–42).

Tusks reach full size when the animal is between around twenty and sixty years of age. Kouyaté may have been male or female, and their tusks continued to grow until they were killed. Their species was most likely *Loxodonta africana*, the African savannah or bush elephant. *Loxodonta* literally means the one with the tooth that is slanting or bent to the side. The tusk of an elephant is a tooth, not a bone as the Arabic etymology would lead one to believe. A histologist would not even call the material "ivory," but rather "dentine." The tusk is the upper incisor composed of dentine, the collagen-infused material that gives its soft texture.

Embedded in the bone sockets of their skull, elephant tusks have the same main physical structures as the teeth of other mammals: cementum; dentine; and a pulp cavity, filled with nerves and blood vessels. We have created a diagram that compares the material composition of a human incisor with that of a tusk

---

[52] For an early twentieth-century photograph of an ivory poacher's caravan fording a stream in the Belgian Congo, see Guérin 2015: 23.

(Figure 27). The sparse hair that grew around Kouyaté's eyes and ear openings grew from the inside outward. Likewise, both Kouyaté's milk incisors, as well as their adult upper incisors, grew from the inside outward. The more they ate during their lifetime, the more dentine grew in their tusk, because food supplied a series of deposits from their nutritional system to all their teeth.

Kouyaté once used their tusks for fighting and defense, and for digging, stripping bark, and breaking branches. The nerve in the middle of the tusk

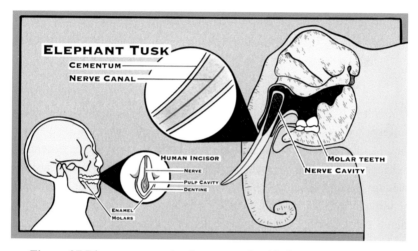

Figure 27 Diagram comparing human tooth with the structure of how Kouyaté's tusk was embedded in the upper jaw, including cementum, nerve cavity, and canal. Photograph: Avery Bonnette.

Figure 28 Elephant tusk cross-section. Nerve canal seen in center.
Source: James St. John, Wikimedia Commons.

extended through the center. A cross-section of an elephant tusk reveals a small hole in the middle throughout the length of the tusk, through which the nerve canal transverses (Figure 28). If the tusk had been removed during Kouyate's life, like any of their teeth, they would have felt pain. Before they were fully grown, Kouyaté had a set of milk teeth and four small molars. During the first year of their life, before it was replaced by the adult tooth, Kouyaté had a small nursing incisor in its place. The hollow (the conical-shaped pulp cavity) is much larger in young animals than older ones. Because of the difference, some art historians have noted that some ivory pieces were made from milk teeth, which were used for inkwells in the Middle Ages. But this was not the case with regard to Kouyaté, who was one of thousands upon thousands of anonymous full-grown elephants killed for ivory.

7 Sunjata

As Kathleen Bickford Berzock, curator at the Block Museum at Northwestern University, writes in *Caravans of Gold, Fragments in Time*, medieval Africa played a significant role in world history because of the far-reaching systems of exchange that crossed through the Sahara Desert. Saharan Africa history, Bickford Berzock notes (2019: 24), "must be accounted for in understanding the world today." For example, in the thirteenth century, the south Saharan Mali empire controlled the commercial center of Audaghost. Imazighen traders would have carried ivory and other goods from Audaghost by caravan across the Sahara to trading points including Egypt, which in turn supplied global markets, including Iberian kingdoms and the Song Dynasty.

By the thirteenth century, large elephant tusks were the preferred source for ivory in China and Spain, as well as many other parts of the world, and ivory originating from the Mali empire increasingly entered the system of global circulation after crossing the Sahara Desert. In the final section of this Element, we examine the African epic *Sunjata* within the context of ivory and elephants in the global Middle Ages. Our hope is that the following material will be useful for those who wish to teach a classic text of African literature alongside the history of global ivory networks and elephants.

Scholars date *Sunjata* to around 1226. There is no way to know for certain when the poem was composed because no written version of the song existed before Djibril Tamsir Niane, a historian and creative writer from Guinea, published a translation of Mamadou Kouyaté's performance. Having learned the song from oral tradition, Kouyaté sang the epic in Mande. Niane translated it to French in 1960 and later translated it to English in 1965.

Mande is a language spoken by the Mandinka ethnic group from West Africa, numbering about 11 million people living in a wide geographical span of the coastal region bordering the Atlantic to the west and southwest, including the modern states of Senegal, the Gambia, and Guinea. The area cuts across boundaries established by French and British colonial administrations, and the people of this region share a common history and culture stemming from a centuries-long sense of affiliation to the ancient, precolonial empire of Mali.

The song has been passed through oral tradition for about eight centuries by the *jeli* (minstrel, bard, or griot), a performer who recites from memory. *Jeliya* is the Mandinka name of the embodied practice of the *jeli*'s profession, in which the performance is made in a chanting mode with added gestures, often accompanied by musical instruments, addressing the story directly to the audience. The community forms part of the performance of *Sunjata* because the audience responds with song, words, or shouts throughout the recitation. The performance mode of the songs to Mary that were collected for Alfonso's *Cantigas* was also a form of medieval oral sung poetry in Spain. In the case of the *Cantigas*, the songs were first collected and written down by King Alfonso in the late thirteenth century. In turn, in the case of *Sunjata*, the epic song was first written down by Djibril Tamsir Niane in the twentieth century.

Several recorded versions of the song exist. The folklorist David Conrod published five original recording sessions at Fadama in northeastern Guinea from the performance by the *jeli* Djanka Tassey Condé. Conrod published another recording from west-central Mali sung by the *jeli* Fa-Digi Sisòko – a recitation that lasts over four hours. Other modern recordings of *Sunjata* include the collaboration between the *jeli*, musicians, and academics in the West. One concert in London in 1987 celebrating music from Mali featured a veteran *jeli* singing *Sunjata* with another musician playing the kora, a stringed instrument with tonal qualities comparable to those of the harp.

A map known as the Catalan Atlas situates *Sunjata* within the global Middle Ages. The Atlas helps provide a possible date for the epic because *Sunjata* is an epic cycle that celebrates Sundiata Keita (1190–1255), prince and legendary founder of the Mali empire. The Catalan Atlas, dated 1324, in turn, depicts Mansa Mūsā I, emperor of Mali, Sundiata Keita's great-nephew. The map therefore helps confirm the scholarly suggestion that the first versions of the epic were already sung in previous generations, including that of Sundiata Keita, before Mansa Mūsā reached the height of his power.

Sunjata celebrates its hero as hunter. In one version recorded in 2014 at Cape Breton University in Nova Scotia, Canada, Chérif Keita provided the poetic translation in English of the version of *Sunjata* in which two master musicians from Mali performed, singer Hawa Kassé Mady Diabaté accompanied by Fodé Lassana Diabaté on the balafon (a gourd-resonated xylophone like a marimba) (Sunjata 2016). The Cape Breton rendition of *Sunjata* begins by celebrating the exploits of Sunjata as warrior and hunter – he is an epic hero because of his prowess with the bow and arrow.

The written version of the epic published by Niane specifies what animal the hero warrior hunts, a detail left out of the 2014 performance. Sundiata Keita was an elephant hunter. In Niane's first rendition of the epic to the non-Mande world, the hero's success is celebrated, in part, through elephant hunting. He wins the affection of powerful witches by offering them each an elephant that he and his companions have killed: "Here, I am returning from the hunt with my companions, and we have killed ten elephants, so I will give you an elephant each and there you have some meat!" (Niane 1989: 26).

The Catalan Atlas provides a representational context for the elephants in *Sunjata* in the interconnected global world of the Middle Ages. Three elephants are depicted on the map: one in Indonesia, a probable reference to a subspecies of the Asian elephant which to this day still dwells in some of its lowland forests; a second elephant is in north central India; and the third is depicted in the central region of sub-Saharan Africa, just east of the depiction of King Mansa Mūsā. In the thirteenth century, princes traded Asian elephants with their mahouts as tribute gifts, but live elephants were not shipped out of Africa. They were hunted, and their ivory harvested. Teachers can examine the witch scene and the hero as elephant hunter in Niane's original translation of *Sunjata* to explore how one element of the epic legend interconnects with the global Middle Ages.

The Catalan Atlas, made in the kingdom of Aragon, provides a visual medieval representation that complements the elephant killing scene in *Sunjata* because its depiction of the African king was created for the European ruler of one of the globe's most significant thirteenth-century trading posts, Majorca. Moreover, the map portrays sub-Saharan Africans in two radically different ways. For instance, one image is unclothed, and the other is regally adorned. Connecting elephants with black bodies, the tusked elephant on the African continent in the Catalan Atlas is depicted opposite a camel and naked Black man in the part of the world map that represents Africa. Maps often labeled Africa in terms related to blackness, following the lead of scholars such as the tenth-century historian, Ibrāhīm ibn Muḥammad al-Iṣṭakhrī, geographer and cartographer of Persian origin, who referred to the region south of the Sahara as the "land of the Blacks" (Bickford Berzock 2019: 24). In contrast to the depiction of the unclothed Black man, the Catalan Atlas portrays Mansa Mūsā I as dressed as a great emperor, holding a large nugget of gold in one hand and a European-style scepter in the other.

The Catalan Atlas depiction of Mansa Mūsā I gives evidence of the reach of the geopolitical scope of the Mali empire in the medieval period. The hero of the Mali epic, Mūsā's great-uncle, kills elephants, providing an example from literature of the ivory that circulated into global markets. In sum, in the same years that China exported what it called the best ivory from Africa and Alfonso and Violante held ivory Madonna icons, and in the same years that the oral histories of the Madonna were compiled into the *Cantigas*, Sundiata Keita's descendants were likely celebrating their hero in the first versions of the *Sunjata* epic cycle.

In this Element, we named the African elephant that provided the ivory for the Spanish Virxe Abrideira statuette "Kouyaté." In the context of elephants in the global Middle Ages, the naming of an animal is not always an act of human domination over an animal, particularly when the individual elephant was nameless and forgotten. "Kouyaté," the name chosen for the elephant whose tusk became the Virxe Abrideira, honors a centuries-long line of oral performers and wordsmiths that identify as the Kouyaté clan. Mamadou Kouyaté, the performer of the first published version of the epic, is not the only person named Kouyaté to sing about elephants. Other performers, such as Tata Bambo Kouyaté, sang "Sama" (Elephant), broadcast on national radio in Mali in 1988 (Schulz 2021).

After consulting Chérif Keita – who not only provided the translation of the poem in the 2014 performance in Nova Scotia but is a descendant of Sundiata and Professor of Africana Studies at Carleton College – over email and on the telephone, we decided to use the name Kouyaté to pay tribute to the family who is keeping alive the African song cycle. In offering material for teaching *Sunjata*, we consider the importance of naming a forgotten elephant. The Kouyaté clan name literally means "there is a pact between us" in Mande. Chérif Keita underscores that the elephant is an animal quality of the Kouyaté family clan, which has several animal qualities or totems. One animal quality is *samaguera*, which literally means the "elephant (*sama*) becoming white (*guera*)." On the one hand, the study of the Mande word *samaguera* can be useful for discussing the history of race with regards to ivory carving in Europe. Elephant tusks traveled in the Gothic century and were transformed into the preferred skin-color choice on holy images.

On the other hand, *samaguera* is useful for considering how an unfamiliar concept, a clan's totem for the elephant, might encourage new ways of understanding human connections with animals as kin, which, in turn, might lead to teaching modules that inspire mutually beneficial human–animal land-sharing practices. Humans were responsible for the extinction of the North African species of elephant, and they have forced Asian elephants into captivity for centuries. In sub-Saharan Africa, however, humans lived alongside elephants in the wild. Teachers can use an elephant-centered pedagogy based on *Sunjata* in its global context to invoke elephant spirits (totems) for learning how humans and animals can better share the earth.

8 Conclusion

Although they are on two opposite sides of the planet, the cases of Spain and China demonstrate that medieval cultures, animals, and people were not as segregated as national-based histories sometimes suggest. This Element has underscored interconnected global ivory-supply networks, particularly the role of Africa as supplier of what was considered the best ivory from the Middle Ages. A slaughtered elephant could have supplied ivory to China or Spain in the thirteenth century because, after being sourced in west or central sub-Saharan Africa, it arrived in Egypt, where ivory loads were put into trade networks flowing east as well as westwards.

Aside from ivory, live elephants were also transported from one place to another in the Middle Ages. The elephants that humans exported, however, were not the African species, but Indian elephants with their mahouts. The Portuguese were responsible for transporting live Indian elephants to Europe at end of the medieval period, but very few live elephants arrived in Europe prior to the fifteenth century. None arrived in Spain in the thirteenth century. In the case of China, in contrast, live Asian elephants regularly moved out of forest regions in Vietnam for a life in captivity in populated cities. They were made captive to serve ritual: howdahs were placed on their backs, and they were adorned for processions, always guided by an individual handler.

A study of elephants and ivory highlights the place of animals and animal products in the history of interactions between cultures. Ivory trade connected Christian Spain with Islamic Spain, as well as northern and sub-Saharan Africa. Elephant tributes formed a basis for Vietnamese diplomacy with the Chinese empire. Intercultural connections did not preclude cultural prejudices: Christian Europe used elephants and ivory as a sign of Islam's defeat, and it developed a beauty-standard preference for ivory-white skin, while it concurrently depicted black skin on its African ivory suppliers. China, in turn, formed an ethnocentric attitude of cultural superiority over Vietnam, which supplied it ivory, elephants, and mahouts. Sources disparagingly refer to the Vietnamese as querulous, lacking refinement, arrogant, and greedy.

A non-anthropocentric approach to history also acknowledges the individuality and dignity of animals who once lived and were killed or exploited by human beings. Paleoarcheological analysis through radiocarbon isotopes of a small sample of ivory from a Chinese stave or the Iberian statuette studied in this Element might provide more information about the elephant to whose tusk the ivory belongs. A sample could help confirm their species, what they ate, and the geography of where they roamed. It could also provide the dates that the animal lived. With regards to the thirteenth century, radiocarbon dating confirmed that the date of one of the ivory sculptures in the Metropolitan Museum of Art, an enthroned Virgin and Child, was an elephant that died between 1210 and 1290 (Little 2014: 14).[53]

Our interest, however, has not been to employ scientific methods in approximating the afterlife of two elephant tusks and the lives of the elephants. In the case of the stave, the ivory tool was ubiquitous, carried by thousands of Chinese administrators in the medieval period. In the case of the statuette, isotopic analysis of the Virxe Abrideira will not be undertaken for the time being because laws about cultural heritage in Spain do not allow samples to be taken from ivory. Ashley Coutu (2015) has observed, nonetheless, that no single line of evidence can create an elephant's life history. Science is a piece of the puzzle for completing an understanding of the life story of the elephants whose tusks were used to create ivory artifacts. In the reclamation of two previously anonymous lives, our study proposed likely hypotheses based on methodological approaches from the humanities, most especially the recuperation of archival documents and cross-disciplinary historical methods.

By the end of the Middle Ages, global trade networks developed further, and more loads of elephant tusks from sub-Saharan Africa were shipped to the east and west. The *Bom Jesus*, a Portuguese trading vessel sunk in the early sixteenth century, was found in 2008 in southern Africa near Namibia. The vessel, whose hull contained over 100 tusks from African elephants, was destined for India, and much of the cargo probably would have been sent to China (de Flamingh et al. 2021). Other Portuguese boats brought loads of ivory to Europe. By the beginning of the 1500s, Lisbon had opened several ivory-carving workshops (Jordan Gschwend and Lowe 2015), and ivory carving became so commonplace in Iberia that a verb for carving ivory (*marfilar*) entered the Spanish language in the early modern period.

In this Element, we seek to look beyond the ivory artifact as "thing" to the dignity of those individual elephants that provided it. African elephants have faced such a threat to their existence from human hunting that they evolved a gene for tusklessness to survive (Campbell-Station et al. 2021). Asian elephants, in turn, share some of the same challenges as African elephants, including threats from habitat loss and poaching. They also, given that a third of all Asian elephants live in captivity, face challenges that all intelligent and

---

[53] An isotope study of a tusk confirmed the range throughout Alaska where an Arctic woolly mammoth roamed, and the different foods it ate (Wooller et al. 2021). The load of tusks discovered in the hull of a sunken sixteenth-century Portuguese ship was determined to be from elephants from the savannah and mixed habitats that surround the Guinean forest block of West Africa (de Flamingh et al. 2021).

emotionally sensitive captives face. They live with captive syndrome in that they desire freedom and at the same time do not want to abandon humans.

Kouyaté and Y Khun, this Element offered a plausible scenario that explains how your tusks came to be used for human purposes in thirteenth-century China and Iberia. You are two elephants in the room for those studying elephant ivory artifacts, and one cannot consider the Iberian statuette or the stave without recognizing you. It is impossible to turn back history to discover the names of the people that turned your tusk into an artifact. Rest assured, though, that some mourn your loss.

But the history of elephants is not only a history of mourning, but also of birth. Y Khun and Kouyaté, your tooth grew as you walked and breathed. It is not difficult to imagine a scenario for your birth. You were both born in the wild among females. In their excitement, heads and ears were held high to the sound of flowing urine and trumpets and bellows. When born, you lay on the ground. One of the females, a mother and grandmother, friend, or cousin, standing in the circle that surrounds you, nudged you to stand up. You, on first try, wobbled and plopped back down to the ground. Your legs flailed as you lay on your side. But the concert of elephant sounds of trumpets grew louder, and another used her trunk to encourage you to stand. Then, twenty minutes or so after breaking from the amniotic sac, you, in the patted-down grasses, stood up again. Amid all the elephant trumpeting, you took a first step.

Notes about the Text

Translations are our own unless otherwise indicated.

Regarding quotations from original Chinese documents, italics indicate notes in smaller typeface, set two lines to a single line of the text, all vertical, read right to left.

In order to save space, Chinese dates are sometimes presented as: reign title +historical year+lunar month+cyclical day. Days, months, and years are often calculated in recurring cycles of sixty, a combination of divisions of the heavens based on the movement of Jupiter, dividing heaven into twelve "stems" and earth into ten "branches"; from a possible 120 combinations, sixty are chosen to represent years and months in a never-ending sexagenary cycle. Since traditional months were divided into three decades, there was a rough correspondence to two months per cycle of sixty. However, since lunar months are either twenty-nine or thirty days long it is not perfect.

Note also that the peripatetic seats of government in China between 1127 and 1138 are as follows:

Yangzhou	November 1127→February 1129
Lin'an (Hangzhou)	February 1129→May 1129
Jiankang (Nanjing)	May 1129→November 1129
Yuezhou (Shaoxing)	May 1130 →February 1132
Lin'an (Hangzhou)	February 1132→October / November 1134
Pingjiang (Suzhou)	October/November 1134→January / February 1135
Lin'an (Hangzhou)	February 15, 1135→September/October 1136
Pingjiang (Suzhou)	September/October 1136→ February 1137
Jiankang (Nanjing)	March 1137→April 1138

References

Primary Sources

Ballesteros Beretta, A. (1934). Itinerario de Alfonso X, rey de Castilla. *Boletín de la historia* 104: 49–88, 455–516.

Cai Tao 蔡絛 (1983). *Tieweishan congtan* 鐵圍山叢談 [Collected Discussions from Iron Wheel Mountain]. Beijing Zhonghua shuju.

Casson, A. (2023). *Cantigas de Santa Maria for Singers*. www.cantigasdesanta maria.com/csm/299.

Clavijo, G. (1782). *Vida y Hazañas del Gran Tamorlan con la descripción de las tierras de su imperio y señorio escrita por Ruy Gonzalez de Clavijo, camarero del muy alto y poderoso señor don Enrique Tercero deste nombre*, 2nd ed. Madrid: Antonio de Sancha.

Dawes, E. A., trans. (1928). *Medieval Sourcebook: Anna Komnene: The Alexiad (English)*. Greek Texts and Translations. https://anastrophe.uchicago.edu/cgi-bin/perseus/citequery3.pl?dbname=GreekNov21&getid=1&query=Alex.%203.

Dutton, B. and J. G. Cuenca, eds. (1993). *Cancionero de Juan Alfonso de Baena*. Madrid: Visor Libros.

Fan Chengda 范成大 (1781). *Hengyu zhi* 衡虞志 [Treatise of the Supervisor of Forests and Rivers and of Marshes and Mountains]. In Xie Weixin 謝維新 (ed.), *Gujin hebi shilei beiyao* 古今合璧事類備要 [Complete Essentials of Past and Present in Perfectly Matched Pairs]. Beijing: Wuying dian.

Fan Chengda 范成大 (2002). *Fan Chengda biji liuzhong* 范成大筆記六種·. Beijing: Zhonghua shuju.

Fan Chengda 范成大 (2010). *Treatises of the Supervisor and Guardian of the Cinnamon Sea*. Trans. J. M. Hargett. Seattle, University of Washington Press.

Orta, Garcia de (1563). *Colóquio dos simples, e drogas e coisas medicinais da Índia e assim de algunas coisas tocantes a medicina prática, e outras coisas boas para saber* (1563), 84. Accessed at *Arquivo Nacional Torre do Tombo*. Lisbon: Instituto dos Arquivos Nacionais. https://digitarq.arquivos.pt/viewer?id=4614066.

Jōjin 成尋 (2007). *San Tendai Godaisan ki shō* 参天台五臺山記上 [Part One of A Record of Visiting Mt. Tiantai and the Wutai Mountains]. Trans. Fujiyoshi Masumi 藤善眞澄. Ōsaka: Kansai daigaku tōsei gakusho kenkyūja.

Jōjin 成尋 (2009). *Xin jiao Can Tiantai Wutai shan ji* 新校参天台五臺山記 [A Record of Visiting Mt. Tiantai and the Wutai Mountains]. Ann. Wang Liping 王麗. Shanghai: Shanghai guji.

Kulp-Hill, K., trans. (2000). *Songs of Holy Mary of Alfonso X, The Wise: A Translation of the* Cantiga de Santa María. Introduction by Connie L. Scarborough. Tempe: Arizona Center for Medieval and Renaissance Studies.

Lewis, M. E. (2003). Custom and Human Nature in Early China. *Philosophy East and West* 53: 308–322.

Li Min 李民 and Wang Jian 王健 (2004). *Shangshu yizhu* 尚書譯注 [Translation of and Notes to the Venerated Documents]. Shanghai: Shanghai guji chubanshe.

Li Tao 李燾 (1985–95). *Xu Zizhi tongjian changbian* 續資治通鑑長編 [A Continuation of the Long Version of the Comprehensive Mirror for the Aid of Government]. Beijing: Zhonghua shuju.

Li Xinchuan 李心傳 (1936). *Jianyan yilai xinian yaolu* 建炎以來繫年要錄 [Record of Important Events from the Jianyan Reign Period Onward, Arranged Chronologically]. Shanghai: Shangwu yinshu guan.

Meng Yuanlao 孟元老(1999). *Dongjing meng Hua lu jian zhu* 東京夢華錄箋注 [Commentary and Notes to A Dream of Hua in the Eastern Capital]. Ann. Yi Yongwen 伊永文. Beijing: Zhonghua.

Niane, D. T. (1989). *Sundiata, an Epic of Old Mali*. Trans. G. D. Pickett. London: Longmans.

Ouyang Xiu 歐陽修 et al. (2002). *Taichang yinge li* 太常因革禮 [Continuing and Changed Rituals of the Court of Imperial Sacrifice]. Shanghai: Shanghai guji.

Pang Yuanying 龐元英 (2006). *Wenchang zalu* 文昌雜錄 [Records of the Chancellery]. Zhengzhou: Daxiang.

Pliny the Elder. *The Natural History, Book XXXIII*. Perseus Digital Library.

Qian Shuiyou 潛說友 (2006). *Xianchun Lin'an zhi* 咸淳臨安志 [Gazeteer of Lin'an of the Xianchun era]. Beijing: Beijing tushuguan chubanshe.

Rothelin Continuation (1859). *Recueil des historiens des croisades: Historiens occidentaux*. II. Paris: L'Imprimerie nationale. https://gallica.bnf.fr/ark:/12148/bpt6k51572g/f14.item.

Shen Yue 沈約 et al. (2018). *Songshu* 宋書 [Documents of the Song]. Beijing: Zhonghua shuju.

Shirley, J., trans. (1999). *Crusader Syria in the Thirteenth Century: The Rothelin Continuation of the History of William of Tyre with part of the Eracles or Acre Text*. Aldershot: Crusader Texts in Translation.

Xu Song 徐松 (2008). *Song huiyao jigao* 宋會要輯稿 [Edited Administrative Documents from the Song]. Taipei: Zhongyang yanjiuyuan.

Torres Fuentes, J. (2008). *Documentos de Alfonso X el Sabio*. Murcia.

Toqto 脫脫 et al. (1985). *Songshi* 宋史 [History of the Song]. Beijing: Zhonghua.

Wei Shou 魏收 et al. (2017). *Weishu* 魏書 [History of the Northern Wei]. Beijing: Zhonghua shuju.

Wu Bin 伍彬 and Hangzhou shi Dang'an guan 杭州市檔案館 eds. (2006). *Hangzhou gujiu ditu ji* 杭州古舊地圖集 [Old and Ancient Maps of Hangzhou]. Hangzhou: Hangzhou guji chubanshe.

Wu Zhijing 吳之鯨 (1980). *Wulin fan chi* 武林梵志. 1609 ed. Republished. Taipei: Mingwen shuyuan.

Wu Zimu 吳自牧 (2001). *Mengliang lu* 夢粱錄. Jinan: Shandong youyi chubanshe.

Zhang Ji 張洁 (2010). Songdai xiangya maoyi ji qi liutong guocheng yanjiu 宋代象牙貿易及其流通過程研究 [A Study of Song Dynasty Ivory and the Process of Its Circulation]. *Zhongzhou xuekan* 中州學刊: 188–191.

Zhou Mi 周密 (2007). *Wulin jiushi: chatuben* 武林舊事:插圖本. Beijing: Zhonghua shuju.

Zhou Qufei 周去非 (1999). *Lingwai daida jiaozhu* 嶺外代答校註 [Collation and Annotation of Responses to Questions about What Lies Outside the Southern Mountain Ranges]. Ann. Yang Wuquan 楊武泉. Beijing: Zhonghua shuju.

Zhu Xi 朱熹 (1992). *Zhou Yi benyi* 周易本義 [Basic Meaning of the Zhou Changes]. Ann. Su Yong 蘇勇. Beijing: Beijing daxue.

Secondary Literature

Anderson, G. D., and M. Rosser-Owen (2015). Great Ladies and Noble Daughters: Ivories and Women in the Umayyad Court at Córdoba. In *Pearls on a String: Artists, Patrons, and Poets at the Great Islamic Courts*. Edited by A. S. Landau. Baltimore: Walters Art Museum, 28–51.

Bango Torviso, I. G. (2010). *La Abridera de Allariz: El imaginario de la Virgen en la sociedad hispana del siglo XIII*. Murcia: Caja Ahorros Mediterráneo.

Bango Torviso, I. G., and M. T. López de Guereño Sanz, eds. (2009). *Alfonso X el Sabio: Sala San Esteban / Murcia, 7 octubre 2009–31 enero 2010* [museum catalogue]. Murcia: Comunidad Autónoma Región de Murcia, Ayuntamiento de Murcia, Caja de Ahorros del Mediterráneo.

Barciela González, V., G. García Atiénzar, J. A. López Padilla, and M. S. Hernández Pérez. (2022). Producción y consumo de marfil en la Edad del Bronce: Cabezo Redondo (Villena, Alicante) como marco. *Cuadernos de Prehistoria y Arqueología de la Universidad Autónoma de Madrid* 48.2: 79–106. https://doi.org/10.15366/cupauam2022.48.2.003.

Barnet, P. (1997). Gothic Sculpture in Ivory: An Introduction. In *Images in Ivory: Precious Objects of the Gothic Age* [exhibition catalogue, Detroit

Institute of Arts and Walters Art Gallery]. Edited by P. Barnet, 2–17. Detroit: Detroit Institute of Arts.

Barrow, R. (2021). Gunhild's Cross and the North Atlantic Trade Sphere. In *The Global North: Spaces, Connections, and Networks before 1600*. Edited by C. Symes. Amsterdam: ARC, Amsterdam University Press, 53–76. https://doi.org/10.1515/9781641894906-005.

Bedini, S. (1998). *The Pope's Elephant*. Nashville: J. S. Sanders and Co.

Berceo, G. (1989). *Milagros de Nuestra Señora*. Edited by M. Gerli. Madrid: Catedra.

Beusterien, J. (2020a). The Black Madonna Icon: Race, Rape, and the Virgin of Montserrat in *The Confession with the Devil* by Francisco de Torre y Sevil. In *Goodbye Eros: Reassessing the Ethos of Love in Age of Cervantes*. Edited by A. Laguna and J. Beusterien. Toronto: University of Toronto Press, 191–220.

Beusterien, J. (2020b). *Transoceanic Animals as Spectacle in Early Modern Spain*. Amsterdam: Amsterdam University Press.

Beusterien, J. (2023). What's in a Name? Animals and Humanities Biogeography. In *A Companion to Spanish Environmental Cultural Studies*. Edited by L. I. Prádanos. Woodbridge: Tamesis, 119–124.

Bickford Berzock, K., ed. (2019). *Caravans of Gold, Fragments in Time: Art, Culture, and Exchange across Medieval Saharan Africa*. Princeton: Princeton University Press.

Bleeke, M. (2020). Ivory and Whiteness. *Different Visions* 6: 1–23.

Carpenter, D. (2020). *Henry III: The Rise to Power and Personal Rule, 1207–1258*. New Haven: Yale University Press.

Caviness, M. (2008). From the Self-Invention of the Whiteman in the Thirteenth Century to *The Good, The Bad, and The Ugly*. *Different Visions* 1, https://differentvisions.org/wp-content/uploads/sites/1356/2020/03/Issue-1-Caviness-2.pdf.

Clutton-Brock, J. (1999). *A Natural History of Domesticated Mammals*, 2nd ed. New York: Natural History Museum.

Cobb, P. M. (2021). *Coronidis Loco*: On the *Meaning of Elephants*, from Baghdad to Aachen. In *Interfaith Relationships and Perceptions of the Other in the Medieval Mediterranean*. Edited by S. Davis-Secord, B. Vicens, and R. Vose. New York: Springer, 49–77.

Coutu, A. N. (2015). The Elephant in the Room: Mapping the Footsteps of Historic Elephants with Big Game Hunting Collections. *World Archaeology* 47.3: 486–503. https://doi.org/10.1080/00438243.2015.1016184.

Cutler, A. (1985). *The Craft of Ivory: Sources, Techniques, and Uses in the Mediterranean World: A. D. 200–1400*. Washington, DC: Dumbarton Oaks Research Library and Collection.

Druce, G. C. (1919). The Elephant in Medieval Legend and Art. *Archaeological Journal* 76: 1–73.

Ebrey, P. (1999). Taking Out the Grand Carriage: Imperial Spectacle and the Visual Culture of Northern Song Kaifeng. *Asia Major* 12: 33–65.

Elvin, M. (2004). *The Retreat of the Elephants: An Environmental History of China*. New Haven: Yale University Press.

Estella Marcos, M. (1984). *La escultura del marfil en España: Románica y Gótica*. Madrid: Editora Nacional.

Ferreira, M. P. (2016). The Medieval Fate of the Cantigas de Santa Maria: Iberian Politics Meets Song. *Journal of the American Musicological Society* 69.2: 295–353. https://doi.org/10.1525/jams.2016.69.2.295.

Flamingh, A. de, A. Coutu, J. Sealy, et al. (2021). Sourcing Elephant Ivory from a Sixteenth-Century Portuguese Shipwreck. *Current Biology* 31(3): 621–628. https://doi.org/10.1016/j.cub.2020.10.086.

Folda, J. (2005). *Crusader Art*. Cambridge: Cambridge University Press.

Franco Mata, M. A. (2006). Liturgia hispánica y marfiles: Talleres de León y San Millán de la Cogolla en el siglo XI. *Codex Aquilarensis* 22: 93–145.

Frei, K., A. Coutu, K. Smiarowski, et al. (2015). Was It for Walrus? Viking Age Settlement and Medieval Walrus Ivory Trade in Iceland and Greenland. *World Archaeology* 47.3: 439–466.

Gaborit-Chopin, D. (1997). The Polychrome Decoration of Gothic Ivories. In *Images in Ivory: Precious Objects of the Gothic Age*. Edited by P. Barnet. Detroit: Detroit Institute of Arts, 46–61.

Galán y Galindo, A. (2011). Evolución de las técnicas de talla en marfil. *Arte, arqueología e historia* 18: 77–106.

Gertzman, E. (2015). *Worlds Within: Opening the Medieval Shrine Madonna*. University Park: Pennsylvania State University Press.

Gertzman, E. (2020). Playthings: Ivory on Ivory. In *Games and Visual Culture in the Middle Ages*. Edited by E. Lapina and V. Kopp. Turnhout: Brepols, 221–237.

González Hernando, I. (2011). *El arte bajomedieval y su proyección: Temas, funciones y contexto de las Vírgenes abrideras tríptico*. Madrid: Editorial Académica Española. www.ucm.es/centros/cont/descargas/documento35755.pdf.

Graff, D. (2000). *Medieval Chinese Warfare*. London: Routledge.

Greenspoon, L., Krieger, E., Sender, R., et al. (2023). The Global Biomass of Wild Mammals. *Proceedings of the National Academy of Sciences USA* 120.10: e2204892120. https://doi.org/10.1073/pnas.2204892120.

Guérin, S. M. (2013). Forgotten Routes: Italy, Ifrīqiya, and the Trans-Saharan Ivory Trade. *Al-Masāq, Journal of the Medieval Mediterranean* 25.1: 71–92.

Guérin, S. M. (2015a). *Gothic Ivories: Calouste Gulbenkian Collection.* Lisbon: London Scala Arts and Heritage Publishers in association with Calouste Gulbenkian Foundation.

Guérin, S. M. (2015b). The Tusk: Origins of the Raw Material for the Salerno Ivories. In *The Salerno Ivories: Objects, Histories, Contexts.* Edited by A. Cutler, F. Dell'Acqua, H. L. Kessler, A. Shalem, and G. Wolf. Berlin: Reimer Verlag-Gebr. Mann, 21–29.

Guérin, S. M. (2019). Gold, Ivory, and Copper: Materials and Arts of Trans-Saharan Trade. In *Caravans of Gold, Fragments in Time: Art, Culture, and Exchange across Medieval Saharan Africa.* Edited by K. Bickford Berzock. Evanston: Block Museum of Art; Northwestern University, 175–201.

Guérin, S. M. (2022). *French Gothic Ivories: Material Theologies and the Sculptor's Craft.* Cambridge: Cambridge University Press.

Harms, R. W. (1981). *River of Wealth, River of Sorrow: The Central Zaire Basin in the Era of the Slave and Ivory Trade, 1500–1891.* New Haven: Yale University Press.

Harris, N. (2020). *The Thirteenth-Century Animal Turn: Medieval and and Twenty-First-Century Perspectives.* Cham: Palgrave Macmillan.

Heng, G. (2018). *Invention of Race in the European Middle Ages.* Cambridge: Cambridge University Press.

Horton, M. (1996). *Shanga: The Archaeology of a Muslim Trading Community on the Coast of East Africa.* London: The British Institute in Eastern Africa.

Iafrate, A. (2015). *The Wandering Throne of Solomon: Objects and Tales of Kingship in the Medieval Mediterranean.* Leiden: Brill.

Ilahiane, H. (2006). *Historical Dictionary of the Berbers (Imazighen).* Lanham: Scarecrow.

Instituto de Historia y Cultura Naval (2016). La marina de la Corona de Aragón: Jornadas de historia marítima. Ciclo de conferencias, octubre 2015. Cuaderno Monográfico 72. Madrid: Ministerio de Defensa. https://publicaciones.defensa.gob.es/media/downloadable/files/links/c/u/cuaderno-72.pdf.

Jackson, P. (2007). *The Seventh Crusade, 1244–1254: Sources and Documents.* Aldershot: Ashgate.

Jordan Gschwend, A. (2010). *The Story of Süleyman: Celebrity Elephants and Other Exotica in Renaissance Portugal.* Philadelphia: Pachyderm.

Jordan Gschwend, A. and K. J. P. Lowe (2015). *The Global City: On the Streets of Renaissance Lisbon.* London: Paul Holberton.

Jordan Gschwend, A. and K. J. P. Lowe, eds. (2017). *A cidade global: Lisboa no Renascimento / The Global City: Lisbon in the Renaissance* [exhibition catalogue]. Lisbon: Museu Nacional de Arte Antiga.

Jung, J. (2010). The Tactile and the Visionary: Notes on the Place of Sculpture in the Medieval Religious Imagination. In *Looking Beyond: Visions, Dreams, and Insights in Medieval Art and History*. Edited by Colum Hourihane. Princeton: Index of Christian Art, 203–240.

Kangwana, K., and C. Browne-Nuñez (2011). The Human Context of the Amboseli Elephants. In *The Amboseli Elephants*. Edited by C. J. Moss, H. Croze, and P. C. Lee. Chicago: University of Chicago Press, 29–36.

Katz, M. R. (2009). Marian Motion: Opening the Body of the *Vierge ouvrante*. In *Meaning in Motion: The Semantics of Movement in Medieval Art*. Edited by N. Zchomelidse and G. Freni. Princeton: Department of Art and Archaeology, Princeton University in association with Princeton University Press, 63–91.

Katz, M. R. (2012). The Non-Gendered Appeal of Vierge Ouvrante. In *Sculpture: Audience, Patronage, and Purpose in Medieval Iberia*. Edited by Therese Martin. Leiden: Brill, 37–92.

Kessler, Herbert L. (2015). Mediatas/Mediator and the Geometry of Incarnation. In *Image and Incarnation: The Early Modern Doctrine of the Pictorial Image*. Edited by W. S. Melion and L. Palmer Wandel. Leiden: Brill, 17–75.

Kistler, J. M. (2006). *War Elephants*. Westport: Greenwood.

Kouyaté, M. (performer) & D. T. Niane (novelization) (1965). *Soundjata ou l'Epopée MandinGuérin*. Paris: Présence Africaine, 1960.

Laguna Paúl, T. (2009). Virgin de las batallas. In *Alfonso X el Sabio: Sala San Esteban / Murcia, 7 octubre 2009–31 enero 2010* [museum catalogue]. Edited by I. G. Bango Torviso and M. T. López de Guereño Sanz. Murcia: Comunidad Autónoma Región de Murcia, Ayuntamiento de Murcia, Caja de Ahorros del Mediterráneo, 22–23.

Laufer, B. (1925). Ivory in China. *Anthropology, Leaflet 21*. Chicago: Field Museum of Natural History.

Levtzion, N. and J. F. P. Hopkins, eds. (1981). *Corpus of Early Arabic Sources for West African History*. Trans. J. F. P. Hopkins. Cambridge: Cambridge University Press.

Little, C. T. (2014). The Art of Gothic Ivories: Studies at the Crossroads. *Sculpture Journal* 23.1: 13–29. https://doi.org/10.3828/sj.2014.3.

Luciañez Triviño, M. (2018). *El marfil en la edad del cobre de la península ibérica: Una aproximación tecnológica, experimental y contextual a las colecciones ebúrneas del mega-sitio de Valencina de la Concepción – Castilleja de Guzmán (Sevilla)*. Seville: University of Seville.

Lu Yun 陸芸 (2014). Tang Song shiqi liuju guangzhou de waiguo musilin shangren 唐宋時期留居廣州的外國穆斯林商人 [Foreign Muslim Merchants Residing in Guangzhou in the Tang and Song Dynasties]. *Xibei minzu daxue xuebao* 西北民族大學學報 4: 50–57.

Malcolm, A. (2022). Long in the Tusk, Then and Now. *Network in Canadian History and Environment | Nouvelle initiative Canadienne en histoire.* https://niche-canada.org/2022/02/09/long-in-the-tusk-narwhals-then-and-now/.

Marinetto Sánchez, P. (1987). Plaquitas y bote de marfil del taller de Cuenca. *Miscelánea de Estudios Árabes y Hebraicos. Sección Árabe-Islam* 36: 45–100.

McCracken, P. (2020). Animate Ivory: Animality, Materiality, and Pygmalion's Statue. Oxford Medieval Studies Lecture, given at the University of Oxford, 23 January.

Metropolitan Museum of Art (1993). *The Art of Medieval Spain, A.D. 500–1200.* New York: Metropolitan Museum of Art.

Mas García, J. (1987). *El marfil en la antiguedad: Seguimiento de sus manufacturas hasta el Suroeste ibérico.* Academia Alfonso X El Sabio.

Medina, A. M. R. (2023). The 'Mutualisation' of Maritime Risk in the Crown of Castile, 1300–1550. In *General Average and Risk Management in Medieval and Early Modern Maritime Business.* Edited by M. Fusaro, A. Addobbati, and L. Piccinno. Cham: Palgrave Macmillan.

Nance, Susan. (2015). *Animal Modernity: Jumbo the Elephant and the Human Dilemma.* Palgrave Macmillan.

Nees, L. (2006). El elefante de Carlomagno. *Quintana: Revista de Estudos do Departamento ds Historia da Arte* 5: 13–49.

Ng, Su Fang. (2019). *Alexander the Great from Britain to Southeast Asia: Peripheral Empires in the Global Renaissance.* Oxford: Oxford University Press.

Ottewill-Soulsby, S. (2023). *Emperor and the Elephant: Christians and Muslims in the Age of Charlemagne.* Princeton: Princeton University Press.

Owner of Vietnam's Largest Tamed Elephant Herd Worries about Elephant Extinction (2015). Vietnamnet Global.

Pardo, M. A., K. Fristrup, D. S. Lolchuragi, et al. (2024). African Elephants Address One Another with Individually Specific Name-Like Calls. *Nature, Ecology, and Evolution* 8: 1353–1364. https://doi.org/10.1038/s41559-024-02420-w.

Paster, G. K. (1998). The Unbearable Coldness of Female Being: Women's Imperfection in the Humoral Economy. *English Literary Renaissance* 28: 416–440.

Patton, P. (2016). An Ethiopian-Headed Serpent in the *Cantigas* de Santa María: Sin, Sex, and Color in Late Medieval Castile. *Gesta* 552: 213–238.

Patton, P. (2022). Color, Race, and Unfreedom in Later Medieval Iberia. *Speculum* 97.3: 649–697.

Pittaway, I. (2018). Surprising Songs of Sentient Statues: The Virgin, Venus, and Jason and the Argonauts. *Early Music Muse: Early Music and Performance*. https://earlymusicmuse.com/sentientstatues-cantigas/.

Rodriguez, A. (2020). Narrating the Treasury: What Medieval Iberia Chronicles Choose to Recount about Luxury Objects. *The Medieval Iberian Treasury in the Context of Cultural Interchange (Expanded Edition)*. Edited by T. Martin. Leiden: Brill, 61–80.

Rosser-Owen, M. (2015). The Oliphant: A Call for a Shift of Perspective. *Romanesque and the Mediterranean: Points of Contact across the Latin, Greek and Islamic Worlds c. 1000 to c. 1250*. Edited by R. M. Bacile and J. McNeill. Leeds: Routledge. 15–58.

Salvador Martinez, H. (2010). *Alfonso X, the Learned. A Biography*. Trans. O. Cisneros. Leiden: Brill.

Schleif, C. (2009). Saint Hedwig's Persona Ivory Madonna: Woman's Agency and the Powers of Possessing Portable Madonnas. In *Four Modes of Seeing: Approaches to Medieval Images in Honor of Madeline Caviness*. Edited by E. Lane, E. Pastan, and E. Shortell. Surrey: Ashgate, 449–474.

Schulz, D. E. (2021). *Political Legitimacy in Postcolonial Mali*. Marltesham: Boydell & Brewer.

Shalem, A. (2004). *The Oliphant: Islamic Objects in Historical Context*. Leiden: Brill.

Shalem, A. (2005a). From Royal Caskets to Relic Containers: Two Ivory Caskets from Burgos and Madrid. *Muqarnas* 12: 24–38.

Shalem, A. (2005b). Trade in and the Availability of Ivory: The Picture Given by the Medieval Sources. In *The Ivories of Muslim Spain: Papers from a Symposium Held in Copenhagen from the 18th to the 20th of November 2003*. 2 vols. Edited by K. von Folsach and J. Meyer. Copenhagen: The David Collection, vol. 2, pp. 25–36.

Shell, J. (2015). *Transportation and Revolt: Pigeons, Mules, Canals, and the Vanishing Geographies of Subversive Mobility*. Cambridge, MA: MIT Press.

Sidebotham, S. E. (2019). *Berenike and the Ancient Maritime Spice Route*. Berkeley: University of California Press.

Silva Santa-Cruz, N. (2012). La espada de Aliatar y dos pomos en marfil nazaríes. Conexiones estilísticas e iconográficas. *Anales de Historia del Arte* 22: 405–420. https://doi.org/10.5209/rev_ANHA.2012.39097.

Singh, D. (1965). *Ancient Indian Warfare with Special Reference to the Vedic Period*. Leiden: Brill.

Somerville, K. (2016). *Ivory: Power and Poaching in Africa*. London: Hurst.

Star B., J. H. Barrett, A. T. Gondek, and S. Boessenkool (2018). Ancient DNA Reveals the Chronology of Walrus Ivory Trade from Norse Greenland. *Proceedings of the Royal Society of Biological Sciences* 285: 1–9. https://doi.org/10.1098/rspb.2018.0978.

Stevenson, W. (2021). *The Origins of Roman Christian Diplomacy: Constantius II and John Chrysostom as Innovators*. London: Routledge.

The Sunjata Story: Glimpse of a Mande Epic. (2016). *The Centre for Sound Communities*. January 9, 2016. www.youtube.com/watch?v=yOS78ul1_rA.

Tao, J. S. 2009. The Move to the South and the Reign of Kao-tsung. In *The Cambridge History of China: Volume 5, the Sung Dynasty and Its Precursors 907–1279*. Edited by D. C. T. Witchett and P. J. Smith. Cambridge: Cambridge University Press, 644–707.

Trautmann, T. (2015). *Elephants and Kings: An Environmental History*. Chicago: University of Chicago Press.

Whitmore, J. K. (1986). "Elephants Can Actually Swim": Contemporary Chinese Views of the Late Ly Dai Viet. In *Southeast Asia in the 9th to 14th Centuries*. Edited by A. Milner. Singapore: Institute of Southeast Asian Studies, 117–137.

Wooller, M. J., C. Bataille, P. Druckenmiller, et al. (2021). Lifetime Mobility of an Arctic Woolly Mammoth. *Science* 373: 806–808. https://doi.org/10.1126/science.abg1134.

Xihu laoren 西湖老人 (pseud.) (1956). Xihu laoren fansheng lu 西湖老人繁盛錄 [A Record of Splendors by the Old Man of West Lake], in Dongjing meng Hua lu (wai sizhong) 東京夢華錄 (外四種) [A Dream of Hua in the Eastern Capital (and four other texts]. Bejing: Zhonghua shuju.

Yu Beishan (2006). 宇北山. *Fan Chengdu nianpu* 范成大年譜. Shanghai: Shanghai guji chubanshe.

Zhang Ji 張洁 (2010). Songdai xiangya maoyi ji qi liutong guocheng yanjiu 宋代象牙貿易及其流通過程研究 [A Study of Song Dynasty Ivory and the Process of Its Circulation]. *Zhongzhou xuekan* 中州學刊 3: 188–191.

Acknowledgments

Thanks to Avery Bonnette, Theresa Flanigan, Connie Scarborough, Abel Alves, Ronny Azuaje, Isidro Bango Torviso, María Beusterien, Carol Blakney, Ashley Coutu, Jesús Llorente de la Cea, Frederick De Armas, Juan Pablo Gil Osle, Sarah M. Guérin, Liz Friend-Smith, Geraldine Heng, Chérif Keita, Paul Lane, Sister María Ángel de la Eucaristía, Julie Couch, Jeremy James McInerney, Susan Noakes, Lynn Ramey, Luis Rodríguez-Rincón, Riccardo Pizzinato, Comfort Pratt, Carlos Sambricio, and Kristen Michelson.

Another hearty appreciation goes out to the students in Medieval and Renaissance Studies Survey courses at Texas Tech University from the Spring of 2021 and 2023.

A special thanks to the many students who have provided inspiration over the years in seminars on medieval China. A special thanks to Yang Shao-Yun for his careful reading of the manuscript and suggestions for improvements.

Cambridge Elements ⹀

The Global Middle Ages

Geraldine Heng
University of Texas at Austin

Geraldine Heng is Perceval Professor of English and Comparative Literature at the University of Texas, Austin. She is the author of *The Invention of Race in the European Middle Ages* (2018) and *England and the Jews: How Religion and Violence Created the First Racial State in the West* (2018), both published by Cambridge University Press, as well as *Empire of Magic: Medieval Romance and the Politics of Cultural Fantasy* (2003, Columbia). She is the editor of *Teaching the Global Middle Ages* (2022, MLA), coedits the University of Pennsylvania Press series, RaceB4Race: Critical Studies of the Premodern, and is working on a new book, Early Globalisms: The Interconnected World, 500–1500 CE. Originally from Singapore, Heng is a Fellow of the Medieval Academy of America, a member of the Medievalists of Color, and Founder and Co-director, with Susan Noakes, of the Global Middle Ages Project: www.globalmiddleages.org.

Susan J. Noakes
University of Minnesota–Twin Cities

Susan J. Noakes is Professor of French and Italian at the University of Minnesota – Twin Cities, where she also serves as Chair of the Department of French and Italian. For her many publications in French, Italian, and comparative literature, the university in 2009 named her Inaugural Chair in Arts, Design, and Humanities. Her most recent publication is an analysis of Salim Bachi's *L'Exil d'Ovide*, exploring a contemporary writer's reflection on his exile to Europe by comparing it to Ovid's exile to the Black Sea; it appears in *Salim Bachi*, edited by Agnes Schaffhauser, published in Paris by Harmattan in 2020.

Lynn Ramey
Vanderbilt University

Lynn Ramey is Professor of French and Cinema and Media Arts at Vanderbilt University and Chair of the Department of French and Italian. She is the author of *Jean Bodel: An Introduction* (2024, University Press of Florida), *Black Legacies: Race and the European Middle Ages* (2014, University Press of Florida), and *Christian, Saracen and Genre in Medieval French Literature* (2001, Routledge). She is currently working on recreations of medieval language, literature, and culture in video games for which she was awarded an NEH digital humanities advancement grant in 2022.

About the Series

Elements in the Global Middle Ages is a series of concise studies that introduce researchers and instructors to an uncentered, interconnected world, c. 500–1500 CE. Individual Elements focus on the globe's geographic zones, its natural and built environments, its cultures, societies, arts, technologies, peoples, ecosystems, and lifeworlds.

Cambridge Elements ≡

The Global Middle Ages

Elements in the Series

Eurasian Musical Journeys: Five Tales
Gabriela Currie and Lars Christensen

Global Medievalism: An Introduction
Helen Young and Kavita Mudan Finn

Southeast Asian Interconnections: Geography, Networks and Trade
Derek Heng

Slavery in East Asia
Don J. Wyatt

Early Tang China and the World, 618–750 CE
Shao-yun Yang

Late Tang China and the World, 750–907 CE
Shao-yun Yang

Medieval Textiles across Eurasia, c. 300–1400
Patricia Blessing, Elizabeth Dospĕl Williams and Eiren L. Shea

The Chertsey Tiles, the Crusades, and Global Textile Motifs
Amanda Luyster

Swahili Worlds in Globalism
Chapurukha M. Kusimba

"Ethiopia" and the World, 330–1500 CE
Yonatan Binyam and Verena Krebs

Global Ships: Seafaring, Shipwrecks, and Boatbuilding in the Global Middle Ages
Amanda Respess

Elephants and Ivory in China and Spain
John Beusterien and Stephen West

A full series listing is available at: www.cambridge.org/EGMA

Printed in the United States
by Baker & Taylor Publisher Services